Ech

When Allie hears
presence of unseen
she doesn't know t
a real-life drama w
years ago. Her researching the area as a holiday project and they can't understand why Allie is becoming increasingly worried and upset. The parallel stories of present-day Allie and Victorian Louisa are skilfully interwoven in this exciting and unusual ghost story.

Gail Renard is a freelance writer and this is her first full-length novel. She lives in London though she is Canadian, and she wrote the original television script as well as the novel.

Echoes of Louisa is based on the ATV networked production of the same name, which stars Lucinda Bateson as Allie/Allegra, Amanda Kirby as Louisa and Jeremy Nicholas as Anthony.

ECHOES of LOUISA

Gail Renard

Beaver Books

First published in 1981 by
The Hamlyn Publishing Group Limited
London · New York · Sydney · Toronto
Astronaut House, Feltham, Middlesex, England
(Paperback Division: Hamlyn Paperbacks, Banda House,
Cambridge Grove, Hammersmith, London W6 0LE)

ISBN 0 600 20433 2

Printed and bound in England by
Hazell Watson & Viney Limited, Aylesbury, Bucks
Set in Times

This book is dedicated to
Dorothy Viljoen
Paul Harrison
and my parents

Contents

1

The Homecoming 1876/1981

The pony and trap turned down the long drive, and Louisa Hallam, looking eagerly about, leaned as far forward as she could, so as not to miss a sight. Rutland was so different from London, and she drank in the long rolling lawns and green budding gardens, which were especially bright that Easter.

'Louisa! Do be careful!'

Louisa turned, and looked at Miss Craddock, her governess who was sitting beside her. She laughed, and pushed herself even farther forward as the house came into view.

Thornaby Hall was more than a house. It was an imposing grey building, all dignity and stone; standing square and erect in its own grounds. Louisa's green eyes sparkled as she surveyed the Hall. She couldn't wait to be in it, especially as Mamma and Papa would be there too.

Louisa never saw much of her parents in London, as they had travelled abroad extensively with her father's career in the Diplomatic Corps. She saw even less of all her brothers and sisters who, mostly older, were either away at school, or in the army, or in the case of the girls, were married.

But it was her parents that Louisa had missed the most, and she was happy at this strange and sudden removal to the country. She smiled as she sat back in her seat, and Miss Craddock patted her hand in approval. The pony and trap drew up before the house, and quickly, before they had stopped, Louisa jumped down.

'Louisa! Louisa, wait until the pony stops!'

But it was too late. Louisa darted about, taking a better look at Thornaby Hall.

'Louisa, you must wait for me!'

Miss Craddock gathered her skirts with a sigh, and came down from the trap as quickly as she could. But Louisa continued to bob about, taking no notice of her harrassed governess.

'Isn't this wonderful?' she cried, running round and about. 'I wonder where the stables are?'

Miss Craddock's normally patient Scots voice sounded strained. She had been with the Hallam family for a long time, almost thirty years, since the birth of their first son Anthony, and right now, she felt her age.

'Louisa, you must not get yourself untidy before you see your Mother!'

But Louisa had at last caught sight of the stables. She was about to dash across to them when Miss Craddock finally managed to catch hold of her. The governess then turned her attention to their driver, who was beginning to unload their baggage.

'Please do be careful with the cases,' she pleaded. 'And don't drop my portmanteau . . . '

As the driver dropped Miss Craddock's portmanteau from the top of the trap, Louisa laughed, and pulled away. She turned and looked again at Thornaby Hall, her eyes shining. Then, picking up her long skirt, and grasping her straw boater, Louisa ran towards the house with a cry. 'Aren't you so, so glad to be here?'

Inside the large front entrance hall of Thornaby Hall, confusion reigned. The mahogany staircase was littered with cases and various chests which servants pushed to and fro. Large white sheets covered what was probably furniture; and the odd trunk blocked people's way in the hall. And in the midst of it all, directing the various servants as a general would his army, stood Lady Margaret Hallam.

Lady Margaret was a small, rather rotund lady, but she made up in volume what she lacked in size. With a wave of her lace handkerchief, she directed her campaign in an excitable manner. She was waving the little tweeny Mary towards the library as the girl pushed an enormous trunk.

'Oh this is too, too much,' cried Lady Margaret. 'Push it over there!'

Little Mary threw her full weight against the trunk, and it shifted slightly. She rested for a fraction of a second to catch her breath.

'No, no, I can still see it!' trumpeted Lady Margaret as she bore down on the tweeny and the trunk. 'Push it over *there*!'

The front door suddenly flew open, and Louisa, as if shot from a cannon, ran up to her flustered mother.

'Mamma!'

'Louisa, child!' Lady Margaret acknowledged her daughter briefly; and looked her up and down. She thought the child had grown since she'd last seen her, though she couldn't be sure. She nodded approvingly at the way her daughter was dressed, in a brown woollen skirt and a sailor blouse. So suitable for a young girl of fourteen. Or was she fifteen? Lady Margaret couldn't be certain. She turned her attention to Harris, the driver, who had just entered with the baggage.

'Take those bags upstairs, Harris. Oh. No,' she said, quickly changing her mind, 'leave them where they are. It's noon. You're to fetch Master Thomas and Master Roderick from the station!'

Louisa screwed up her face in surprise. Thomas and Roderick! Were they coming too? And she had so looked forward to being alone with her parents!

Lady Margaret busied herself with the remaining footmen and bags; taking little notice of Louisa. She wished the child wouldn't pull her face like that. But Louisa was persistent.

'But why are *they* coming? It's not their end of term yet!'

Lady Margaret looked around the vast hall vaguely. Where *were* those gladstones; the ones she had last seen in

King's Cross station? Possibly still there . . .

Louisa followed her mother about, waiting for a reply.

'Mamma!'

Miss Craddock suddenly hurried through the front door, clutching her now battered portmanteau. Lady Margaret spotted her gratefully.

'Miss Craddock; take Louisa upstairs and get her settled as quickly as you can! Mary will show you to your rooms'.

'Yes, Your Ladyship.' Miss Craddock attempted to steer Louisa towards the staircase. But Louisa resisted.

'No!' she cried, her green eyes flashing. 'I want to go to the stables! I want to see the pony Papa promised me!'

Lady Margaret took Louisa to one side and said with great difficulty and patience, 'Papa has had other . . . *things* . . . on his mind just now . . .'

She wavered for a moment, lost in thought. Then she quickly brightened.

'But if Papa promised you a pony; I'm sure it will be here . . .' She looked about the hall and the mess; a bit dubiously. 'Somewhere . . .'

Lady Margaret turned her attention back to Mary, who was balancing a cricket bag in each hand.

'And Mary! Don't forget to see to the . . . *extra room.* Oh, my!'

Lady Margaret was suddenly overcome. Her fluttery handkerchief flew to cover her mouth. She hurried towards the library, as Miss Craddock shepherded Louisa up the stairs.

'Come quickly Louisa.'

Louisa was totally confused. 'But *why*?'

But Miss Craddock just prodded Louisa gently up the stairs, handing the overladen Mary her portmanteau to carry.

A tearful Lady Margaret flew into the library, where she found her husband, Sir Reginald Hallam, pulling rather angrily on the bell sash for the servants. She tried to retrace her steps, quickly.

'Margaret!'

Sir Reginald swiftly approached his wife. He was a stern man, seldom in the best of humours. Though impeccably dressed in brown frock coat and silk cravat, his temper was ruffled; and his manner was as stiff as his high starched collar. Lady Margaret was easily flustered.

'Oh, please don't ask me! I'm sure I don't know where anything is! Or anyone!'

Sir Reginald ignored her as always, and turned back to his bell. He'd been ringing for ages, and wanted the carriage. Where *was* Harris?

Lady Margaret's heart sank as she remembered she'd sent Harris to fetch the boys. She wondered if her husband had intended to meet Anthony, who would be arriving back in England that day. It wasn't every day their eldest son resigned from the army. But somehow she doubted it, because Sir Reginald hadn't seen Anthony off when he had departed, and that was a far happier occasion.

'Shall you be meeting the boat?'

'Certainly not!' Sir Reginald rounded on his wife angrily. 'How could you even ask?' Anthony's resignation was looked upon as a disgrace.

He gave the bell sash another tug, and Lady Margaret was glad that she wasn't the bell sash.

She turned away, rather shaken. 'Oh, I'm sorry. Only as I thought as it's really no distance at all . . . it would be such a pleasant trip . . .'

Sir Reginald glared at his wife, then busied himself with some papers on his desk.

'Margaret, kindly don't concern yourself!'

Lady Margaret became even more shaken and flustered. She turned back to her husband, a bit too brightly. 'The boys should be here soon. Thomas and Roderick! Won't it be lovely to have them here with us?'

Sir Reginald looked at his wife, askance. Only Lady Margaret could think it charming to be forced to remove one's sons from Uppingham in the middle of a term, and ruin their chances in a trice. He supposed that she would say next that she was glad that he had given up his career, and their London life; and all because of their eldest son. Sir Reginald turned away in annoyance.

Lady Margaret made one last attempt at communicating with her husband.

'It's just that everything has happened rather quickly . . . What with the lack of servants – half of them gave their notice. And all that moving from London. I shan't be near any of my friends . . . And they shan't want to see us anyway . . .' Lady Margaret faltered 'It's all been such a strain . . .'

She suddenly felt faint. She looked round for a chair that would hold her weight. She couldn't decide on one quickly enough.

'Oh!'

Sir Reginald looked up from his papers, distracted. He saw his wife starting to sway, and rushed over to steady her.

'Margaret!'

Sir Reginald helped Lady Margaret into a chair, an embroidered one, but it was too late. She had swooned. He rushed to tug at the bell sash, but there was no reply. He pulled even more furiously.

Where were those blasted servants when you needed them?

Louisa flew into the nursery, with an admonishing Miss Craddock and a laden Mary struggling behind on the stairs. The tiny room was full of boxes and crates. A small brass bed, covered by a white lace counterpane, stood in one corner, and a large rocking horse seemed to take up the rest of the room. A washstand with pink wash jug and basin, and a small chest of drawers huddled along the opposite wall. But being so happy to be in the country, Louisa greeted it joyfully.

'Louisa, don't run!'

Miss Craddock and Mary entered behind Louisa. Mary put down the luggage, and gratefully left the room, while Louisa bobbed about, examining every nook and cranny.

'Is this to be my room?'

Miss Craddock closed the door so as not to disturb the rest of the household, and started to organise the bags. But Louisa turned up her nose as she sighted first the rocking horse, and then some toys.

'But it's for an infant! I'm fifteen years old now!'

She tossed her long brown hair indignantly, and began to remove the various dolls and games she came across on the shelves. Miss Craddock followed Louisa about, replacing the toys that Louisa had displaced.

'I'm sure it can all be changed later. Now I think you should have a rest.'

Miss Craddock went to turn down the cosy brass bed for Louisa. It looked inviting, but Louisa refused its offer. She decided to unpack some of the bags.

'Where are my combs?'

Miss Craddock was tired, and tried to keep her Scots temper under control. They had only just arrived.

But Louisa had already prised open another bag, and tossed aside a couple of cricket pads with reckless abandon.

'That's not mine! Nor that!'

Miss Craddock caught the pads as Louisa tossed them to one side. But Louisa had now pulled out a couple of cricket bats as well. Miss Craddock didn't fancy being walloped by them. She descended upon her charge.

'Louisa, all that will be seen to later! Everything is rather topsy turvy just now! But we must try and settle down!'

Louisa obeyed Miss Craddock by opening one last box. She tilted it so she could peer inside.

'What's in here?'

Miss Craddock hurried over to Louisa as she saw the box beginning to tip over. But it was too late. A boxful of books cascaded onto the floor. Miss Craddock despaired as Louisa picked up a book, and pulled a face.

'School-books?!'

* * *

Allie Burr watched as her father, Roger, tried to find the turn-off on the motorway that would lead them to the county that used to be Rutland. Patience was never her father's strong point, and never more so than when the entire family were yelling directions all at once. Allie, being sixteen and wise, decided to take a passive approach, and settled back snugly in her anorak and woolly cap to watch the rolling hills, and the green and budding trees, and the speed restriction signs which sped before her.

Roger thrust the AA handbook at his wife, Fran, who was sitting beside him in the car. As Fran peered at Roger through her sunglasses, and wrapped herself more snugly in her sheepskin coat, Allie realised that her mother would be of little help. Fran liked to treat road maps as an adventure, and Roger wasn't going to have any of that, not when facts were required. Roger passed the handbook to the back of the car, where Allie sat with her younger brother, Shaun. Shaun grabbed the handbook before Allie could take it, and studied it upside down. Allie sighed. This was going to be some Easter holiday!

Allie tried to ignore Shaun, who fancied himself a clown, and wondered aloud why their father wanted them along on his history project in the first place.

Roger answered her boomingly, as if he were still addressing his students at the college.

'It'll do us good to participate in a project together! And I might even get my research done in half the time!'

Allie doubted that. No one in the family had ever done

on-the-site research before, aside from Roger. She doubted that Shaun had even read a book. But Roger chose to ignore all that.

He smiled at his daughter through the rear view mirror.

'And besides, who know's what we might learn?'

Allie still seemed dubious, but Shaun looked out of the window and smiled. He had just learned something very useful indeed.

'Dad, we've just gone past our exit!'

'What?'

Roger jerked his head outside his window, and saw that they had indeed passed the turn off for Rutland. Allie thought she saw one or two new grey hairs being added to the crop already on her father's head. Shaun laughed, and Fran tried not to smile as Roger concentrated on searching for the next exit.

The Burr's Easter holiday had definitely begun.

The Burr's car roared up the Rutland village street, and finally ground to a halt. Roger had no sooner switched off the engine than Fran and Shaun got out and ran towards one of the local shops.

Roger and Allie left the car at a more leisurely pace.

'You'll enjoy this, you know. History's not all leaping about with Magna Cartas and maps!'

He paused to have a quick look around.

'History's about dealing with recent events too! And local ones!'

Allie looked around the sleepy village, and then up at her father.

'But *Rutland* . . . ?'

Roger leaned against the car which was overloaded with boxes and suitcases. He tried not to knock over a portable telly which was resting on top.

'Yes, Rutland! That's my point exactly!' he said, looking for his pipe. 'We shouldn't be popping off to prehistoric places when we've got important cultural events right here on our doorstep!'

Allie sighed as Roger lit his pipe. He puffed away. 'After all, Rutland as a county is no more! Just think of all the interesting changes we're going to find! Think of the local history we can absorb! And I want to share all of this with you!' Roger smiled at his daughter. 'And besides, I got a grant for it.'

'I see.' Allie looked off in the direction where her mother and brother had gone. Roger continued.

'And more to the point, we don't spend nearly enough time together as a family. Sometimes I think I don't see nearly enough of you! Or your brother!'

Roger gave Allie a little hug. She glanced up at him with a smile. That wasn't always such a bad thing!

Roger ignored that. 'But I'm hoping this holiday will change all that. I'm hoping that from now on, we'll be able to act as one. That this should bring us closer together!'

He suddenly looked around.

'Now where have your mother and brother gone?'

Allie pointed in the opposite direction to which Roger had started walking.

'It's this way, Dad!'

Roger stopped suddenly, and reversed. And he and Allie walked into one of the little village shops.

In the clutter of the village shop, Fran was battling with the telephone while Shaun handed her five-pence pieces. Roger and Allie went to join them.

'Any luck?'

Fran shook her head; the receiver poised for another call. She was running out of possibilities and five-pence pieces. The pips on the phone suddenly sounded, and Fran snatched another five pence from Shaun. She fed the phone, and then waited. 'Oh, hello?'

Roger, Allie and Shaun moved away to give Fran some

more room. Shaun looked up accusingly at his father, and voiced what they were all thinking.

'Why haven't you booked a hotel?'

Roger looked down at Shaun with disdain, and then remembered that he was only thirteen. 'Hotel? Who do you think you're related to; an Arab? No, we'll just find a guest house or something; there's no need to book!' Roger had really got going now. Shaun was sorry he had asked. 'Besides, that's the whole point to our holiday! To share new experiences, to rediscover family life; all the joys of adventure! Don't you have any of the Baden-Powell boy-scout spirit left in you?'

Shaun kicked against one of the shop's displays. 'I'm bored.'

Roger looked at his son in surprise. 'Already?'

Shaun continued with his usual lack of charm. 'And it's getting late. *And* if we have to travel much more, I'll be carsick!'

Fran put her hand over the phone. 'I think I've found something—'

Roger hurried over and grabbed the receiver. Without asking whys or wherefores he quickly took it.

The Burrs' 1980 estate car pulled up suddenly outside a ramshackle, neglected cottage; with a screech of brakes and rattle of baggage.

'Everybody out! Here we are!'

Roger, Fran, Shaun and Allie poured out of the car, and stared at the forsaken cottage in amazement.

'I told you we should have booked.'

'Nonsense Shaun! This is much more fun!'

Fran's voice dropped as she turned to face Roger. 'He's right; you should have booked!'

Roger glared, and started unloading their bags from the car. 'There's nothing wrong with this . . . this . . .'

'Hovel?' supplied Shaun cheerfully.

Roger shifted his glare to Shaun. '*Cottage!*'

'That tearing down wouldn't cure!' Shaun finished for him.

Allie stared at the cottage, being careful not to touch anything. The place would have to be rebuilt before it could be knocked down, she thought with a shiver.

Roger struggled with the bags, waiting for his family to finish. But Shaun suddenly looked up towards the roof of the cottage, and shouted in horror. There was no television aerial! Shaun felt withdrawal pains.

Roger passed by Shaun with some bags, secretly glad he might not have to put up with 'Top of the Pops' this holiday. He kicked the front door open. It was time to go in.

'Must we?' asked Shaun.

Shaun was dragged in through the open doorway by his father.

The inside of the cottage looked as bad as its outside.

'Oh my heavens,' breathed Fran, her normally smiling face clouding up.

The Burrs were faced with a single small room, with a number of camp beds, and a cooker and a sink older than time itself. Dirty crockery was piled high in the sink, and the cottage also boasted a rickety old table with four unmatching chairs which were covered by dust and cobwebs. The cottage was dingy and dark, and resembled a Chamber of Horrors.

'All the comforts of home!' noted Roger cheerfully as he set down the bags.

'Whose home?' demanded Fran as she tried to stop him. 'We can't stay here!'

Roger looked around enthusiastically. 'This place just needs cleaning!'

'Razing,' muttered Fran darkly, gazing around.

'I refuse to rebuild any of these walls!' declared Shaun.

Allie merely looked on in horror.

'Will you listen to the lot of you!' cried Roger. 'Do you know what the matter with us is? We've become softies! Slaves to creature comforts!'

Roger ignored the reactions. 'Besides, your mother should know this area quite well. She was born here—'

'Only just,' Fran denied quickly. 'My family moved away when I was *three*!'

'A hundred years ago!' added Shaun. 'When this cottage was first condemned.'

Roger made his decision.

'There's nothing for it. It's getting late. We'll have to spend the night. And if you still don't appreciate this place in the morning; we'll find somewhere else.'

Allie sighed, resigned, and finally spoke up.

'Then we'd better get our things.'

Roger smiled at his firstborn. Now that was his girl!

Allie smiled back.

'Creep!' called Shaun.

Roger and Fran started out to unload the car; but Shaun looked about, and then stopping suddenly, grabbed Allie. 'Allie, wait! Where's the electricity; and the power points?'

Allie had a quick look around. There were none. Shaun was appalled.

'Then how are we going to watch television?'

'By candlelight,' answered Allie as she hurried from the cottage.

* * *

The candlelight and the gaslight flickered faintly in the front hall at Thornaby Hall as Louisa silently made her way down the staircase in her long linen nightdress, over which she had hastily thrown her grey woollen wrap. She had heard her father returning to the Hall and she wanted to ask him about her promised pony. She froze as a clock struck eleven, and had only dared to risk a few more steps when suddenly she was caught from behind.

'What are you doing out of bed at this hour, you naughty girl?' whispered Miss Craddock. 'You must go straight back!'

Louisa strained to break Miss Craddock's hold but it was no use. Miss Craddock had had many years of practice.

'Sh! You will wake your brothers!'

'And get *you* into trouble because you can't control me!' Louisa suddenly stopped struggling. She had heard something outside.

'Listen!'

They strained to hear. Louisa was finally able to break free. It was the carriage and pair. Someone was arriving! She had to see.

'Louisa!'

Louisa had dashed down the stairs before Miss Craddock could catch her. But before she reached the bottom, the front door opened. A soldier, blond, handsome and boyish, in full Hussars' uniform, entered and stared around him. Louisa stood still on the stairs, amazed.

'Anthony?'

Captain Anthony Hallam looked up at Louisa, first in disbelief; then his blue eyes smiling. 'Poppet?'

Louisa flew down the stairs to give her brother a hug.

'I thought you were in India!'

Anthony looked at Louisa and laughed. It was the first time he'd felt like laughing since he had returned to England. 'And I should have thought *you'd* be upstairs in bed!'

He swung the ecstatic Louisa off her feet just as the library door opened.

'What's all this commotion out here?'

Sir Reginald stepped stiffly out into the hall, Lady Margaret timidly following. Sir Reginald hardly saw any cause for celebration.

'Mamma!'

Anthony moved forward to greet his mother warmly. Lady Margaret accepted his kiss, though she tried not to look as though she enjoyed it. It wasn't much use. Sir Reginald glared anyway. Anthony turned and held out his hand to his father.

'Sir.'

Sir Reginald turned, avoiding the outstretched hand. He sharply addressed Miss Craddock, asking her to take Louisa back to bed at once.

Miss Craddock nodded, and hastily took Louisa by the arm. As a very reluctant Louisa was dragged away, Anthony called gently after her.

'Goodnight, Poppet.'

And Lady Margaret burst into tears.

It was late at night as Sir Reginald paced in his study. Anthony, still in his scarlet uniform, was polite though tired, and stood to attention as his father raged.

Anthony cocked an eyebrow as he looked at his father. 'Mamma's looking well.'

Sir Reginald had stopped his pacing. He wondered at his son's coolness.

'If only you knew what all this is doing to her!'

Anthony remembered his father's temper, and answered more stiffly and formally. 'I'm sorry if I've hurt Mamma.'

Sir Reginald rounded on him. Anthony's mother wasn't the only one who had been hurt.

'You don't seem to realise! I've had to sell my London house; remove your brothers from their school, and "retire" to *Rutland.*' Sir Reginald stood before his son. 'And what of your military career, eh, sir?'

Anthony seemed a bit surprised. He had been in the Hussars for ten years now. He was entitled to retire on half pay.

Sir Reginald's voice filled with scorn. '*Retire*? Are you

now? And what of the time and money I've invested in *you*?'

Anthony tried to choose his words carefully. 'I'm very tired, Father; I've had a very long journey. Do you mind if I smoke?'

Sir Reginald exploded. He had never minded what his son had done, that was evident, but couldn't he keep his private live private? Angrily he faced his son. 'There'll have to be a formal apology, of course!'

Anthony looked up from the cigarette he was lighting. 'Apology?'

Sir Reginald's face was as red as Anthony's tunic. 'Do you think you're on some sort of holiday?' Sir Reginald was astounded. He didn't understand his son.

'Perhaps you think you've nothing to apologise for?!'

Anthony was adamant now too. 'No, I don't. Not to the public at large at any rate!'

Sir Reginald grew even more enraged. He had never been so angry with one of his children. But then again, he didn't see them all that often. Perhaps that was just as well. 'You see nothing wrong with recent events?'

'Papa—'

Sir Reginald turned and faced his son furiously.

'Oh, put out that damned cigarette!'

Miss Craddock waited in the dark hall outside the study; her plain woollen dressing-gown wrapped around her for warmth, and her long greying hair in a plait behind her. She shivered a bit as she heard the angry voices coming from within. The door opened suddenly, and then Anthony stormed out, his interview with his father over. Miss Craddock moved eagerly forward, and greeted young Master Anthony. Anthony turned, and looked at her coldly. She continued in a rush.

'I should say *Captain* Anthony. It's so good to have you back!'

Anthony looked wearily round the hall, and made his

way towards the stairs. It was sad that Miss Craddock was the only adult who should be glad to see him. Miss Craddock followed him, chattering.

'Did you have a good crossing? You're looking well. Would you like me to take you to your room?'

Anthony turned on his old nanny. He was not part of her nursery now. He was used to making his own way.

Miss Craddock looked hurt. Anthony was immediately sorry. He had always been fond of her.

'I apologise, Craddie. I didn't mean to snap.' Anthony remembered the manners she had taught him in the nursery, and spoke to her more warmly. 'How are you?'

Miss Craddock looked at Anthony, and formally nodded her reply. She shouldn't have been so familiar. He was an officer now, and no longer her charge. But she had been so happy to see him. Anthony had always been her favourite.

Anthony looked at her kindly. 'Are you well, Craddie? Are you really?' His warm smile melted Miss Craddock even further. 'I am glad. But you'll be wanting to go to your bed now. We can talk in the morning. But I'm glad to see you.'

'Welcome back, sir.'

Anthony escorted his old nanny up the stairs.

* * *

Roger Burr felt ancient as he added yet more suitcases to the growing pile in the crumbling cottage. It looked as though they had crossed an ocean. What a way to start a history expedition!

Fran joined Roger, carrying the portable telly. 'It was *your* idea, darling.'

'To stay here?' wearily admitted Roger.

'To have children,' replied Fran as Allie and Shaun entered, fighting. Allie gladly broke away from Shaun, and approached her father.

'Dad? How do you propose to find out about Rutland? And your history?'

Roger was as surprised at the question as Allie was herself. But she thought as long as the family were to be stuck here, she ought to make the best of it. Besides, she loved her father. Roger dropped the suitcases gratefully, and answered her question.

'Empirically!'

Roger began to explain before Allie could wonder what it meant. It seems that they were to start looking into local facts and records; and visit local houses, to try to collect some historical evidence and facts for themselves. But only one fact interested Fran.

'We need food!'

They had passed an open food shop on their way up from the village, but nobody had bothered to get any food. Roger looked at his wife impatiently.

'Never mind that, Fran,' he complained. 'They're getting interested! I'll get my notes!'

It was as if Roger had said a magical word. Shaun headed for the door.

'Shaun!' bellowed Roger.

'I'll get him!' cried Fran, glad to follow Shaun out. She'd had quite enough of Roger's notes for now.

Roger looked at Fran as she fled. He wondered how he could have married such a Philistine. But his spirit couldn't be dampened for long.

'This is the life, eh Allie? Just think of all the things we'll discover about Rutland!'

Allie watched as Roger went for his notes. She didn't mind helping in the research, but she had hoped to do other things as well. She brushed her wavy light brown hair out of her eyes.

'Won't there be anything else we can do around here?' she asked as she looked round the dismal cottage.

Roger turned back to Allie, surprised. He never thought

of his children as leading their own lives. Besides, what more could Allie want? There were avenues to explore, and mountains to climb!

Allie's sixteen-year-old mind quickly told him. 'Couldn't we go to a film? Or a disco? Just for a break?'

Roger snorted as he placed a mountain of papers before her. There obviously weren't going to be many breaks. Because Roger had their days all planned out.

'After all, what are we here for?'

'Fun?' answered Allie weakly.

'No, we're here on holiday, and to participate in my project! What could be more fun than that?'

Allie debated whether or not she should tell him, when Fran came back into the cottage, thoroughly chilled to the bone.

'Shaun says he's going to the shops.'

Allie's mind worked quickly, and she seized her anorak and her opportunity at the same time. 'He won't know what to buy! I'd better go with him!'

Roger was appalled. He hadn't shown her his notes yet. But Allie rushed out the door.

'I can see them later!'

Roger watched from the window as both his chances of continuing his history empire dashed away. Fran came and stood by him sympathetically. Roger turned to her for help.

'Fran! Now they're both getting away! Say something!'

Fran waved happily from the window.

'Goodbye!'

Allie raced to keep up with Shaun, who was now intent on bringing home the bacon, as well as the eggs. He called to Allie to hurry. He was hungry.

He was *annoying*, Allie firmly decided as at last she caught up with him. She stopped on the path to catch her breath, when suddenly she was struck by a strange and imposing house in the distance. It was a large house, like some big old manor, with one or two of its downstairs lights still shining, and its chimneys smoking. The house was almost the colour of the smoke itself; grey and stony; and it stood quiet and erect, with an almost knowing and unreal appearance, undoubtably caused by its veil of smoke and the fading light. Allie had not seen too many houses like it; not in her native Putney, and she gazed at it, transfixed.

'Come on! I want my dinner!'

But Allie didn't move. She looked at the house's large gardens, and its stables, and thought for a moment how keen her father would be to see it. But the night was drawing in, and Allie finally turned and called to Shaun. But as Allie looked, no one was there. The lights suddenly went off in the manor in the distance, and she was hit from behind by the full force of a loaded carrier bag. Allie heard Shaun's laugh.

'Got you, Dumbo!'

And Allie raced off after Shaun, who ran away laughing, and clutching his carrier bag. Brothers!

* * *

Late next morning, Anthony knocked on Louisa's nursery door. He had been so looking forward to seeing his little sister again; he had missed her.

'Good morning. Louisa?'

Receiving no reply, Anthony entered the nursery. He looked round at his sister's still unmade bed, and smiled at the dolls and toys on display on the shelves. But before he had been in the room for a minute, he had heard the sounds of his youngest sister approaching. Anthony quietly crossed the room, and slipped behind the door. Louisa entered.

'Ah! My prisoner!' cried Anthony, as he caught her from behind. 'Obviously a Punjabi spy!'

Louisa laughed as she spun round to look at her brother,

who was still in his silk dressing gown, though everyone else had long since dressed. Louisa's questions were short, and to the point.

'How long are you staying? What did you bring me?'

Anthony released Louisa, his eyebrows raised. He knew how to handle younger brothers and sisters. 'Bring you indeed! A slap for being so impudent!'

'I'd rather have a present.'

Anthony studied his pretty sister carefully. She had grown so much since he had last seen her. It wouldn't be long until she was a young lady.

'Well, there just might be a present. *When* I unpack.'

Louisa pulled on Anthony's arm, and teased him. 'Unpack now!'

She looked up at her brother. Was it something to wear?

'Yes,' replied Anthony, starting out. He was going to have his bath. Louisa hesitated for a moment, and then ran after him.

'I'm glad . . .'

Anthony stopped, and waited for the show of affection he had been hoping for. Louisa rushed to him.

'I'm glad to see you, Anthony!' She gave her brother a large hug. 'Truly I am.'

Anthony kissed the top of her head. 'Thank you, Poppet,' he replied. 'Did you miss me?'

Louisa nodded her head vigorously. The others weren't nearly so much fun. And they didn't spoil her as much. She would gladly trade all the rest of her brothers and sisters for Anthony.

Anthony seemed thoughtful for a second. 'Is Papa awake yet?'

Louisa nodded her head. Papa had been round and about for hours. Louisa didn't mind, but Anthony seemed to care. He started out of the room. Louisa stopped him.

'Never mind about Papa! Tell me about India!'

'Later!' Anthony wanted to bath and dress before he saw

his father. He didn't want Sir Reginald to see him still wandering about in his dressing gown so late. Louisa began to pout.

'But I want to show you my pony!' Papa had given it her that morning. 'As soon as you're ready!'

'In my own time,' said Anthony smiling. 'I'm a Captain! I outrank you!'

He gave Louisa a wink, and started out of the nursery. Louisa called after him, frustrated.

'But my pony hasn't even a name yet! What am I to call it?'

'Patience!' cried Anthony as he disappeared.

Louisa stamped her foot in annoyance. Now that she had Anthony back, she didn't want to let him go. Miss Craddock entered the room. She read the ill humour on Louisa's face, but decided to ignore it.

'Ah there you are! You should be in the schoolroom! Come along!'

Louisa stood her ground and refused. Miss Craddock looked at her charge, surprised.

'But what is this? Even though we are not in London, you must continue with your education. Like a clever little lady! And there is to be a surprise!'

Louisa felt she could do with a surprise, and was momentarily distracted. She wanted to know what it was. Miss Craddock was steadfast.

'Come along and you shall see!'

Louisa followed Miss Craddock down the long stairs towards the schoolroom. Miss Craddock spoke to her brightly.

'Now that we are in the country, your Mother did not want you to be too isolated, too much alone. So she has invited the young daughter of an old friend to join us. You will be charming, yes?'

Louisa looked around as they entered the schoolroom. She would reserve her opinion. Miss Craddock looked at her with a smile.

'Louisa Hallam, I'd like you to meet Miss Allegra Turner.'

And waiting sedately in the schoolroom, a young girl stood up to meet them. She curtsied.

'How do you do?'

Louisa looked at the girl. She looked about sixteen, and was smartly dressed in a well-cut fawn coloured dress with velvet trim. A silver brooch clasped the lace on her collar, and a tortoise-shell comb held back her long and curling light brown hair. She was attractive, and self-confident, and smiled at Louisa. She was also, although Louisa did not of course know, a Victorian double of Allie Burr.

* * *

2

The Meeting

Allie Burr yawned and stretched; then pushed her pretty chestnut hair out of her face, and looked around. It had taken her quite a full minute till she could remember where she was.

She surveyed the dismal cottage sideways, from her camp bed. The room was strewn with Burr bags, clothing and food, and Allie still shuddered when she looked at it. How she yearned for the privacy of her own room, with her own books and records and posters! Then she heard some grunts and groans, and saw signs of Fran and Shaun beginning to stir. Allie got herself up with a sigh. She decided to try and be bright. The things one did for one's parents!

Allie, Fran and Shaun sneaked up on the sleeping Roger. All were carrying pots and pans, and they approached the head of their family with revenge in their eyes.

'All together now,' whispered Fran. 'On the count of three. One, two . . . *three*!'

'Good morning!' they all screamed, banging their pots and pans as loudly over Roger's sleeping head as they could.

Roger jumped up fitfully, his rickety camp bed shaking beneath him. His blankets slipped onto the floor as they had done a hundred times that night. He looked up groggily.

'He moved!' reported Shaun happily.

Roger remembered where he was. He attempted to focus. He vaguely saw Allie. 'Where's my coffee?'

'In the jar,' said Allie, holding it up for his benefit. 'We've got an electric kettle. And *no* electricity!'

Shaun hovered over Roger cheerfully. 'But we're going

to start a fire as soon as we remember how. Sleep well?'

Shaun didn't bother waiting for an answer. He and Allie dispersed, their fun for the day over. Fran said brightly. '*I* slept like a log!'

Roger started to moan and looked at his bed. He felt as if he had slept *on* a log. Roger suddenly caught sight of his son, who had plopped himself down in front of the portable telly, and was now staring at the blank screen.

'But there's no electricity!'

'That's all right,' answered Shaun. 'There are no programmes on yet!'

'Isn't this fun,' Fran said as she approached Roger, suspiciously happy. 'I was woken by a cockcrow at 5 a.m.!' She smiled at Roger. 'Of course that was nothing compared with being chased by a mouse, or having to fetch *that* washing-up water out of a typhoid infested well!'

Roger choked on the water he was drinking.

Fran looked up at Roger and glared sweetly.

'I wonder whose idea this was anyway?'

Allie and Shaun came to join her. They answered quickly.

'Not mine!'

'Not mine!'

Roger looked at them weakly. 'Mine?'

'Yes!' cried Fran. 'And all because you wanted to go on an historical hunt! Get him, kids!'

Allie and Fran and Shaun jumped on Roger.

* * *

Miss Craddock smiled at her charges, preparing to leave the schoolroom. 'Now Louisa, Allegra, I know you two will become friends.'

She turned away, and Louisa stuck out her tongue behind her back. Miss Craddock did not turn around.

'Louisa, you would prefer to go straight to the schoolroom?'

Louisa smiled sweetly, and linked arms with Allegra. 'No, Miss Craddock, I want to talk with my new friend.'

Miss Craddock nodded and left the room. Louisa released Allegra's arm and started walking about the room, playing with the ornaments.

Allegra surveyed her new schoolmate. Louisa seemed much younger than she was; although Allegra's Mamma had told her that Louisa was all of fifteen. She decided that it must be the way that Louisa dressed; in a rather childish style, in a simple lawn skirt and blouse, and with ribbons in her hair. Her blouse wasn't even lace trimmed. Allegra was lucky that she had her mother's good taste and dress sense to guide her. She unconsciously patted the lace on her collar. Then she noticed that Louisa was staring at her too.

'Hateful, isn't she?'

Allegra seemed rather surprised for a moment, and then realised that Louisa was talking about her Miss Craddock. Allegra said vaguely that she thought she was kind.

'Don't you believe it!' Louisa smiled at her mysteriously, and then noticed the silver brooch pinned to Allegra's dress. Her eyes lit up. Allegra noticed, and unpinned it so Louisa could see. Louisa took it, smiling.

'You've only just arrived, haven't you?' Allegra looked at her new classmate kindly, wanting to chat. 'You didn't mind your having to leave?'

Louisa was examining the brooch eagerly. Of course she didn't. Why should she? She looked up at Allegra, but Allegra remained silent.

'My eldest brother's just come back from India!' Louisa informed Allegra happily.

'Yes–I know.'

Louisa turned round. 'How did you know?'

Allegra leaned forward, in confidence. She had been used to chatting with her sisters, and it was pleasant to be able to share female talk again. 'I heard your Mamma tell my Mamma. *And* that your other brothers were sent back from school.'

'Oh, *them.*' Louisa dismissed Thomas and Roderick. Brothers were such a bore, aside from Anthony.

Allegra followed her. 'Your parents came to dine. They were ever so upset. Aren't you curious?'

Louisa felt uncomfortable, and annoyed, but she was not sure why. And she didn't particularly want to know. 'There's nothing to be curious about!'

'Your Mamma cried.'

Louisa answered softly, more to herself. 'Did she?'

'And your father was cross and cursed!'

'Why should I believe you?' Louisa spun around angrily. She felt hurt and confused. This new girl seemed to know a lot. If she was so clever, who was to be the teacher, Miss Craddock or her? Louisa's green eyes flashed.

'You know, I don't think I want lessons with you! I think you're a silly goose! Catch!'

Louisa threw the silver brooch she'd been fingering back to Allegra. She missed it, and the brooch smashed against the stone of the fireplace. Allegra was about to retrieve it, but Louisa came closer and closer.

'*And* you're a rabbit at catching! A goose *and* a rabbit!' Louise was becoming quite furious now. Allegra's large blue eyes looked puzzled, and she attempted to break away. She didn't know what she had said.

The schoolroom door opened, but Louisa still followed Allegra, oblivious to everything except her own anger.

'I *was* going to invite you to see my new pony! But perhaps now I think you had better stay away! Geese and rabbits are frightened by ponies!'

Anthony stood in the open doorway, his dress uniform vivid in the dull room. He looked at his sister in surprise. He had never heard her speak in such a way, and he didn't like it.

'Louisa!'

Louisa saw her brother, and gratefully ran towards him. But Anthony stopped her short.

'I think you owe your friend an apology!'

Louisa looked at her brother in surprise. Allegra was not her friend, and Louisa knew that she would never be. Surely Anthony would understand that?

Anthony snapped, losing his temper, 'Louisa! We're waiting!'

Louisa saw that Anthony was angry. She turned to Allegra, and apologised with great effort. But it only made her hate Allegra all the more. But Anthony seemed pleased. Louisa had done as he had ordered. He tried to retrieve the situation, and gave both the girls a smile.

'Come along now, you two. Let's find your Miss Craddock.'

Allegra hurried to this handsome soldier's side as quickly as she could. She had had quite enough of her new schoolmate. She had determined not to come back, but Anthony smiled at her as they reached the door.

'And if you're so keen on horses, you must see the new hunter I'll be getting!'

Allegra smiled as Louisa glared.

Louisa entered the conservatory through the garden door, having given Miss Craddock and Allegra the slip. She wanted to speak to Anthony, and had seen him come in here. Anthony was sitting with his sketchbook on his knee, and he was sketching. In the morning light, and amongst all the fresh green plants, Anthony looked much younger than his twenty-eight years. Louisa approached him tentatively.

'Are you still cross?'

Anthony looked up, and saw his sister.

'Shouldn't you be at lessons?'

'Yes.'

Anthony smiled as he studied his sister. He used to get

away from Miss Craddock too. He cleared away some of his papers, and made room. 'No, of course I'm not cross, Poppet. Come and sit by me.'

Louisa settled down on the ground, by Anthony's feet, relieved. She couldn't bear it when he was angry at her. Anthony produced a small box from his pocket.

'But if you're hiding from Miss Craddock, I don't know if I should give you *this*.'

Louisa was immediately tempted. 'Oh, what is it?'

'Guess!'

She thought it might be an elephant, but Anthony said she wasn't even close. She flashed her green eyes charmingly at her brother.

'What else do they have in India?'

Anthony handed her the box. 'Have a look.'

Louisa opened the box, and pulled out a most beautiful silver linked bracelet. She was quite thrilled.

'I told you it was something to wear. Like it?' Anthony moved towards the bracelet teasingly. 'Or I shall take it back . . .'

Louisa pulled away from him laughing.

'No! How wonderful! Allegra *will* be envious!'

Anthony laughed and returned to his sketchbook. 'Manners?'

Louisa threw her arms around Anthony, and gave him a peck on the cheek. She looked over his shoulder to see what he was drawing. He was making a rough sketch of the various plants in the conservatory, and was quite pleased with it. But Louisa was curious.

'What's that you're scribbling?'

'Sketching,' Anthony corrected. 'But go on talking.'

Louisa began hesitantly to apologise to Anthony. She was sorry about her earlier behaviour. She hadn't meant to lose her temper. But it was all so beastly—

'Yes, you were,' said Anthony for once agreeing with her.

Louisa immediately flared, angry at being once again misunderstood. 'I wasn't talking about *me*! I meant that horrid girl Allegra!'

Anthony smiled at her good-naturedly, and gave her his usual answer. 'I'm only concerned with *you*.'

Louisa persevered, trying to make Anthony see sense. She tried to explain the things that Allegra said to her. There was so much she wanted to say. Then she looked at Anthony, and broke off impatiently. He was still sketching.

'You're not listening! Put that away!'

Anthony sketched on, trying to concentrate on an intricate bit.

Louisa flicked her hand impatiently towards his sketch.

'Why are you wasting your time with that?'

Anthony finally stopped, annoyed. 'Charming! Where have you developed such a temper lately? You used to be so sweet!'

'And *you* used to be polite!'

'I'll not take that from you!'

'Then why should I take that from you?'

Anthony and Louisa glared at each other angrily; each with their father's temper. Anthony quickly stood up, and held the door open for Louisa.

'Right my girl; back to your lessons!'

Louisa rushed out into the garden, slamming the conservatory door in a huff.

* * *

Allie was furious as Shaun jumped into a puddle in the middle of the cottage floor.

'Who's for a paddle?'

'Shaun! Stop that! I'll swing for you!'

Allie tried in vain to get out of Shaun's way, but she only succeeded in backing into her mother, who was trying to mop up the flood on the floor. Fran looked at her wearily.

'Don't swing for him in here, dear. There's not enough room for a cat. And don't jump about so much, Shaun! Remember the walls of Jericho! And they were much sounder than these!'

Roger looked up from where he was trying to trace the flood. He wished Fran wouldn't exaggerate. There was nothing wrong with these walls. It was the pipes that were up the spout.

Allie looked to him for help. 'Dad, you promised that if we didn't like this place, we could move!'

Roger answered his daughter as he tried to bandage a pipe. 'But it's so convenient!'

'For running water!'

'For studying Rutland! We're doing an important bit of historical research here!' Fran looked up from her mop, and Roger shut up very quickly.

Shaun grew tired of his puddle. It had been fun at the start, but he'd done that now. He began to follow Allie about.

'Shaun, stop following me!'

Shaun addressed Allie indignantly. 'I'm not! There's just nowhere else to go!'

'I hear there's a quarry nearby,' said Allie darkly.

'Is there?' asked Roger. 'Then we must all go and have a look!'

Allie was immediately exasperated. She wasn't used to such togetherness. She grabbed her anorak.

'I think I'll go for a walk.'

Shaun was immediately at her heels, wanting to go too.

Allie continued on her way outside, slamming the door in her brother's face.

Allie decided to head back towards the large manor house she and Shaun had seen last night. She wanted to get a better look at the place in the light, and perhaps see what had so fascinated her in the dark.

It was one of the few paths she already knew; she enjoyed it. It was such a pleasure to walk along the country lane without having her brother trailing along behind her!

Allie ventured closer to the large house than she had last night. Nobody was about, so she wandered through the large garden, enjoying the sights and the scents and the silence. But the silence didn't last long. Suddenly she heard the sound of a muted door slam, coming from the direction of what appeared to be the old conservatory. Allie looked, saw no one about, but thought she could see a wind rustling through the garden. Then just as suddenly, she saw a ginger-haired man with a rake, as he approached her carrying a sack on his shoulder.

'Are you lost then?'

Allie stared up at him. 'No, I'm just looking. Is that all right?' She was quick to explain that her family was staying at the cottage.

The man, whom Allie guessed to be the caretaker, nodded slowly. 'Are they now? Then look all you want. It's free. Though I shouldn't think there's a lot to see.' The caretaker sighed. 'Except me. I'm the last sight.'

Allie smiled as the caretaker stooped to collect some litter from the ground. He fumbled. Allie immediately sprang forward.

'Here! Let me help!'

She looked round at the Hall and its grounds.

'My father will love all this!'

The caretaker raked up the rubbish, unimpressed. It took all kinds . . .

'He's doing some research. He's studying Rutland!'

'That shouldn't take very long. Seeing that Rutland doesn't exist any more.'

Allie followed the caretaker as he raked away. 'But that's what he's studying. The changes!'

'Been only one change so far as I can see,' the caretaker said passively.

'What?' asked Allie eagerly.

'My postal address.' The caretaker looked at Allie's disappointed face. He tried to be more helpful. He supposed this area had as much history as most.

'Has it?'

The caretaker nodded his head. 'But don't ask me what!'

Allie was suddenly distracted by the sound of Shaun calling her in the distance.

'Allie! Allie!'

She remained silent. The caretaker turned to her.

'Is that you?'

Allie nodded, and hid behind a nearby potting shed. The caretaker was perplexed.

'Aren't you going to answer?'

'No!'

But no sooner had Allie shaken her head than she was swooped down upon by an out-of-breath Shaun.

* * *

The footman lit the lamps in Thornaby Hall as Allegra and Louisa waited by the front door. Louisa wandered about quite lively, as Allegra fretted by the door.

'Where's my Fraulein?'

Louisa stopped as she passed Allegra, and smiled at her sweetly. So Allegra had a Fraulein for a governess, and she had a Scot. They were being educated by a crowd of foreigners!

Louisa was amused at Allegra's discomfort, but Allegra wasn't. She stared out of the hall window, impatiently. Allegra wasn't used to being kept waiting.

'My Fraulein was supposed to call for me before now.'

Louisa sympathised. 'I know; isn't it vexing? Still, it gives us more time together.'

She moved closer to Allegra, and Allegra felt rather sorry she'd offended her before. She tried to make amends. 'I didn't mean to upset you, you know. I hope you weren't—'

Louisa picked up a sweet dish from a nearby table. She didn't wish to hear any hollow words. She offered it to Allegra.

'Chocolate?'

Allegra shook her head, Louisa helped herself. She stared out of the window with Allegra. 'I hope your Fraulein hasn't forgotten about you!'

Louisa picked up an ornament, and started to finger it. Allegra was beginning to look worried. Louisa was glad. Louisa didn't like her. She warmed, and started playing with Allegra as a cat would with a mouse.

'Do you know,' she gushed, 'that if she *had* forgotten about you, and no one knew, you could be a prisoner. *My* prisoner!'

Louisa looked at Allegra with glee. She was starting to look as miserable as Louisa had felt that morning. But before she could enjoy it, the door from the library suddenly opened, and Anthony, splendid in evening dress and black satin cape, stepped out into the hall.

He was rather surprised to find both girls there. It was too late for lessons. He smiled at them both, and asked the reasons for the long faces.

'I think my governess has forgotten to call for me,' answered Allegra.

'Has she? Then perhaps *we* can call for her!'

Allegra looked surprised, but Anthony explained. He was going into Oakham anyway. If Allegra would tell his driver where she lived, he would see her home. 'It's no trouble!'

But it troubled Louisa. She didn't want Anthony to see Allegra home. She didn't want Allegra to have a moment more of Anthony's time than she had herself. She stepped forward.

'Oh that won't be necessary—'

But Anthony had already opened the door. He smiled at Allegra.

'Are you ready?'

Allegra nodded eagerly, more than happy to be away. And she rather looked forward to being with this dashing soldier. Anthony held out his arm. Allegra took it gladly.

'We'll be off then,' he announced. 'Your carriage awaits!' Anthony turned, and smiled a farewell to his sister. He then escorted Allegra out the door.

Louisa had no intentions of ever sharing Anthony with Allegra again. Jealous and enraged, she smashed the ornament she'd been fingering against the polished front door.

'So you've finally found your way home?'

It was more a statement than a question as Sir Reginald strutted about the tea table, fuming. Lady Margaret poured out the tea as Anthony slouched rather morosely in a chair.

'After gallivanting around until all hours in the morning! This is England you know; *not* India!'

Lady Margaret spoke, a bit too brightly and too loudly for Anthony.

'Speak up Anthony! Your Papa is perfectly right!' She passed a plate of rich cream cakes under his nose. 'Cream-cake?'

Anthony tried not to feel ill. Lady Margaret noticed, and was immediately concerned.

'Oh, have you a headache, my dear boy? Would you like a powder?'

Anthony declined politely but Sir Reginald descended upon him once more.

'Couldn't you wait at least a *little* before starting out on your latest exploit? Haven't you given the countryside *enough* to gossip about?'

Lady Margaret joined in. 'After all; this wasn't how you behaved in the army, was it dear boy . . . ?' Lady

Margaret's handkerchief suddenly flew up to cover her face. 'Oh, yes it was . . .'

Anthony moved forward to comfort his mother before she could begin to cry.

'I'm sorry, Mamma.'

Lady Margaret suddenly brightened. She had had a marvellous idea. Perhaps since the army life no longer suited Anthony, he'd be able to follow in his father's career – in the Diplomatic Corps!

Having a scatterbrained wife as well as a negligent son was more than Sir Reginald could bear, even at teatime. He exploded.

'I hardly think he qualifies!'

Lady Margaret's face fell as she reached for her handkerchief again. She was about to sniffle when the maid came in with a fresh pot of tea. The Hallams waited until the maid had left; then Anthony painfully tried to start the conversation again.

'It's not that I didn't enjoy my army career,' he began.

'As you've made only too plain!' Sir Reginald interrupted.

Anthony sighed and started to light a cigarette. He had wanted to tell his parents how much he missed his regiment, missed the fun and the responsibility of his army life, but what was the use? They wouldn't listen. Sir Reginald continued his attack.

'We just want to know what you intend making of yourself! You've left the army; abandoned your career – what surprise have we to look forward to next?'

Anthony knew the answer for himself. 'I'm happy just to have some time to think and sketch.'

Sir Reginald looked at his son with incredulity and dismay. 'Think and sketch? What are you – an *aesthete*?'

Anthony was offended, which made his head hurt even more. He sat up straight, and with all his military bearing faced his father.

'No! I'd just like to do a bit more painting!'

Lady Margaret looked up as she poured yet more tea. She smiled at her eldest son. 'Constable's *Haywain* is such a nice picture, don't you think? Why don't you paint that?'

Anthony stared at his mother, speechless. Sir Reginald had no such complaint.

'We just want you to know that we will not be putting up with any more of your irresponsible behaviour! It's time you learned to pay the piper! You've disgraced this family enough!'

Sir Reginal came and stood next to Anthony's chair. He bellowed for Anthony's benefit.

'Do I make myself clear?'

Anthony felt his head split. For the first time, he rather regretted his late night. He answered his father.

'Very, Papa.'

Sir Reginald drained his teacup, and set it down on the table with a bang. He then slammed out the room.

Anthony's hand flew for a cigarette. As he lit it, his mother moved closer. She proffered the plate of cakes, which now seemed even richer and gooier, and pressed it under Anthony's nose.

'Eclair?'

Anthony hastily excused himself from the tea room.

Anthony strolled, frustrated and alone, out near the stables. The air had done his head some good, but he had begun to regret that he had returned to his parents.

Suddenly he heard Louisa call to him from the distance, and he looked up to see his sister, sporting her new black riding habit complete with top hat, riding her pony towards him. He stopped and waited and managed a smile.

Louisa drew her horse up near him.

'What do you think of my new pony?'

Anthony looked at the pert little chestnut pony, feigning innocence. 'What pony?'

Louisa sat on her pony, bewildered for a second, and then she realised she was being teased. She gave her brother a look, as Anthony walked round the pony, and patted it.

'It's a fine pony, Poppet. What have you called it?'

Louisa sat on her new horse proudly. 'Papa wanted me to call it Discretion or Sobriety, but those are such silly names, don't you think?'

Anthony felt rather strongly about it. 'Yes!'

Louisa had a sudden thought. 'What was *your* horse called in the cavalry?'

Anthony looked rather taken aback. But he quickly answered.

'*My* mount? He was called Turk.' Anthony relaxed for a moment, remembering his army days. 'He was a grand horse.'

Louisa interrupted him, triumphant. 'Then Turk it shall be! Or perhaps Little Turk!' Louisa suddenly looked worried. 'Do you think *she'll* mind?'

Anthony laughed as his sister's face clouded up. 'Not a bit.' He looked at her, kindly. 'Have you finished riding for the day? We could take a walk.'

At this moment Anthony felt he should like to talk with Louisa. But Louisa quickly gathered up the pony's reins.

'No, I want to show you what *my* Turk can do!'

She straightened her hat, then gave her pony a kick to start. Anthony watched her ride off with a sigh.

'Hold her head up!'

But Louisa was out of earshot, and oblivious to everything except her pony. Anthony watched for a moment, then slowly made his way back towards Thornaby Hall.

* * *

The Burrs bounded along towards the large manor house in the distance; Allie enjoying the beautiful countryside and the sunshine more than she thought she would. Fran and Shaun, as always, walked in front, laughing and joking as they strolled. Roger was struggling with his Pentax camera.

'Just look at it!' Roger said, viewing the landscape through the lens of his new camera. 'Just think, this was once a prestigious county, with a history all its own!'

As the stately old Hall came into view, Roger looked at it and enthused. 'What a fine old specimen of Georgiana!' He was by now in full flow. 'Look at that stonework, and those noble stables!'

Allie looked at the Hall and wasn't sure what he meant.

'We're lucky to have a chance to study these places while they're still around!' Roger went on. He stopped and contemplated the old Hall. 'Because it's sad—'

Roger suddenly noticed that the rest of the family had walked ahead without him. Nobody was listening. He dashed to catch up, and faced them disgruntled.

'Thanks a heap!'

Fran looked up at Roger. 'You've seen the house; can we go home now?'

The children brightened and Roger looked appalled. Home? They hadn't even begun to look!

He turned to Allie. He thought at least *she'd* be interested!

Allie looked up at the house, and answered simply. 'I've been here before.'

Roger looked curious, so Allie explained. She told him she'd seen the caretaker. Roger was visibly pleased, and excited.

'Good girl! And what did you find out?'

'Nothing.'

Roger sighed. Educating this lot was going to be an uphill struggle.

Fran looked at the great fortress of a building doubtfully. She didn't fancy scaling the mortar and stone. 'Are we going to break in?'

'No initiative you; that's your problem! What's to stop us from knocking on the door, and asking to speak to its present owner?'

Fran was appalled. 'Propriety! Roger, no!'

Roger sighed once more. His wife stood fixed as he proceeded.

'I'm not going anywhere! I'm just a spectator!'

Roger turned his glance to his children, a bit more hopefully. They were doubled up with laughter.

Shaun and Allie had gone to read a sign which was posted on the property. Their parents gathered round. Roger wanted to know what was so funny.

'That!' said Shaun as he stood holding his sides. The elder Burrs glanced at the sign as Shaun joyfully read, 'Thornaby Hall. Home of the Local Water Board!'

Fran joined her children, and laughed away with glee. Roger looked at the sign with contempt. Thornaby Hall was owned by the council now.

Changes in Rutland home life!

* * *

Dusk was drawing in as Anthony entered the conservatory in Thornaby Hall through the garden door. It was his favourite room, because of its light and airy feel, its array of greenery and plants and because not many people in the house used it. Its vibrant colours and light furniture reminded him of India. He picked up his sketchbook, and was about to perch on a wrought iron bench when he suddenly noticed Allegra, who was reading in the corner. He went and joined her.

'Not out on a pony?'

Allegra looked up quietly and smiled. She told him she'd rather read than ride.

Anthony sat beside her on a garden chair and laughed. There were days in the Cavalry when he'd felt the same.

'Is that why you left?'

Anthony stopped laughing. He looked at Allegra, and then said, 'I was in the army a long time. Almost since I came down from school.'

He was quiet for a moment, his blue eyes thoughtful.

Allegra was curious. 'Were you in many battles?'

Anthony shook his head. He answered quietly. 'For the most part I was lucky. I got to do exciting things like taking care of 'H' troop's baggage in Lucknow!' He shook his head again and laughed. 'And I'll have you know, I was a *Captain*!'

'Didn't you do anything else then?'

Anthony nodded, warming to his subject. 'Oh yes. Took part in a lot of manoeuvres. War games. We used to take each other prisoner.'

He chatted on, thinking of another life. He was reminiscing quite happily now, but not necessarily for Allegra. There was another time when they had presented a horse to Queen Victoria. Anthony remembered the event fondly. It was just before they'd sailed.

'It was a good regiment. We received a commendation. Granted, it was after I left. But it was still a commendation.'

He sighed, lost in a world three thousand miles away. He missed it. Then he became aware of Allegra again. She looked at him with her impenetrable blue eyes.

'If you miss it so much, why don't you go back?'

Anthony looked surprised, and then laughed.

'For the same reason I can't even return to London right now.'

Allegra didn't understand. Anthony merely shook his head. It was never wise to dally with a lady who had dallied with a Prince, especially the Heir . . .

Anthony suddenly jumped to his feet. 'But dammit it all, I don't see why I *shouldn't* go up to London now! What difference could it make?'

Anthony remembered that the totally bewildered Allegra

was with him. He was immediately contrite.

'Oh, I'm sorry.' Anthony looked off through one of the conservatory windows.

'I wonder what Louisa is up to now?'

And hearing Louisa call in the distance, Anthony started off outside, Allegra following.

They found Louisa, with Turk, back in the stables. Louisa pouted the moment she saw Anthony enter.

'Where were you? You were supposed to be watching me ride!'

Anthony looked about at the harness and saddles and stalls in the stable.

'In *here*?'

Louisa looked at Anthony, then burst out laughing fondly. As Anthony listened to Louisa's laugh he was lost in his own thoughts again.

* * *

Roger and Allie and Fran and Shaun examined the grounds outside Thornaby Hall, passing the old stables, completely lost. Roger was still rabbiting on, as they looked for an entrance.

'This is just the sort of significant change I've been talking about!'

Allie looked at her father wearily.

'Yes, but can you find your way inside?'

Roger looked blank, then admitted defeat. Fran was far more helpful.

'Let's go round the back. That might be the way in now.'

'What if there's a side entrance?'

They all looked at Shaun, who had just made the first valuable contribution of his life. They decided to split up.

'We'll try the sides,' decided Roger. 'Kids, you go round the back.'

Shaun disappeared round the Hall out of sight. Allie smiled, and quickly ran after him, passing the old stables as she dashed. And before she had gone very far, she heard a strange laugh. She stopped dead in her tracks, and looked around.

'Shaun?' she called. 'Is that you?'

Allie searched around, but Shaun wasn't anywhere to be seen. Nor was anybody else. Once again, Allie heard the strange, faraway sound.

The laugh seemed to be coming from the deserted stables.

3

The Secret

Roger and Fran finally found their way inside the large entrance hall of Thornaby Hall. What used to be the front door was now permanently bolted, and its little vestibule was now used for the coats, boots and umbrellas of the Water Board workers. They had made their way in through a side entrance.

The front hall had greatly changed since Victorian times. The room looked bare, with lino on the floors, and stark strip lighting, and there was the odd 'Save It!' poster, and a map on the wall. Fran and Roger looked about. There was no one in sight. No one, until Shaun sneaked up on them from behind.

'Shop!'

They jumped.

'Shaun!' exclaimed Fran, as she tried to get her heart restarted, 'where did you spring from?'

Shaun looked around the empty hall. He smiled up at his mother. 'Find anything out yet?'

They were suddenly joined by a man who came out of what was once the library. Roger turned to him and smiled.

'Oh hello! Could you help us? We're trying to trace a family!'

The Burrs all converged on the Water Board worker, as the poor young man instinctively backed away.

Mr Mayhew sat at his desk in Thornaby Hall's former schoolroom, surrounded by Roger, Fran and Shaun. The Water Board man was an awkward, nervous, shy sort of man, and his meeting with the Burrs was only making him more so. He nervously opened a file drawer, the Burr's eyes upon him.

'Now what's the name of this family you want?' he started politely.

'We don't know,' replied Roger. 'But it's the last family who used to live here.'

'Before it ceased to be a private home,' added Fran.

'About one hundred years ago,' finished Shaun. 'More or less.'

A nerve in Mr Mayhew's cheek began to twitch. He looked at them, careful not to turn his back.

'Are they presently paying water rates?' Mr Mayhew asked.

Fran looked hesitant. She doubted it.

Mr Mayhew closed the files gratefully. 'Then I don't really see how I can help!'

Roger leaned across the desk. Mr Mayhew started a bit.

'We know this is unusual,' began Roger. Mr Mayhew nodded his head. 'But we're rather keen to know. It's for our study. To trace various local families, and their histories!'

Mr Mayhew stood his ground. His records didn't go back nearly that far.

Fran looked at him pleadingly. 'Perhaps you could check?'

Mr Mayhew looked dubious, but slowly got up from his desk, and made his way to locate another colleague, who might be able to help. Roger turned round, excited.

'Fascinating, isn't it? You never know what might turn up in an old deed, or bill of sale, or by word of mouth . . .'

Mr Mayhew silently slid his way back to his seat.

'Hallam.'

Roger looked at him. 'Pardon?'

Mr Mayhew faced the Burrs, and tried to look in control. 'The family who last owned the Hall. Hallam.'

Roger was more than pleased. Now they were getting somewhere! Mr Mayhew sighed. Roger rolled on. 'Now. Are there any Hallams still living in the area?'

Mr Mayhew was afraid that he'd ask that. He returned to

his files. Hallam . . . Hallam . . . He looked up at the Burrs and smiled. 'Sorry, no Hallams!' Roger looked disappointed, and was about to say something. Mr Mayhew anticipated it, and quickly jumped in. There weren't any more files!

The Burrs deflated, as Mr Mayhew looked triumphant. 'But might I suggest something? Have you looked in our church?'

Roger sprang up, elated. 'Yes of course! My very next step! Where else do people go in their hour of need?' The Hallams must have been a prominent family! There must be some records of them there!'

'Unless they didn't attend the local church,' helped Shaun. 'Unless they were Jewish.'

Roger exploded. 'Oh ye of little faith! You don't hear Allie nitpicking, now do you?' Roger looked around. 'Allie? *Allie*?'

The Burrs noticed for the first time that Allie wasn't with them. They quickly gathered themselves up, ready to go.

How could they have lost Allie?

The family rushed out from the schoolroom, leaving a mystified Mr Mayhew sitting there, stunned.

Roger poked his head back through the open door. 'Oh, thank you very much. Goodbye!'

And he slammed the door to Mr Mayhew's office in his haste.

Allie stood alone, outside the deserted stables, from where she had heard the laugh. She ventured nearer.

'Hello? Is anybody there?'

She went up and peered into a dusty stable window. And looking inside, she saw nothing but boxes and crates, and various files stored there by the Water Board. Bewildered, she started to open the door when she was caught from behind. She began to struggle, and turned around to see that it was – Shaun. He laughed at his sister as she jumped. 'You scare great! We've been looking for you! Come on! I'll race you back!'

Shaun raced back towards the Hall. Allie took one last look about, then followed.

* * *

Louisa stood by the open door of the stable, laughing and teasing her brother.

'Oh come on, Anthony! Let's go for a ride!'

Anthony stood there, strangely silent, as if he were not really with Louisa or Allegra. Louisa stamped her foot impatiently.

'Anthony! You're not paying attention!' She stole a quick glance at Allegra. 'Or at least not to *me*! Why don't you get your horse and come with me?'

Anthony came out of his dream. He looked at Louisa and the sky outside. It was far too late.

Louisa was peeved, and quickly threw down the reins of her pony.

'You never do anything that I ask!'

Anthony was suddenly very tired, and a bit irritated. He wanted to return to the conservatory, and be alone. He turned and faced Louisa.

'Why don't you play with Allegra? Before she has to go home.'

Louisa ignored that suggestion. She had a new thought, and turned away from Anthony and Allegra happily.

'Where are the boys? I think I'll look for them!'

Anthony was rather surprised. He had supposed that his brothers were visiting some neighbours, at the Grange.

Louisa answered absently, not really interested. They had been sent back. She didn't think that they were welcome there any more. She smiled wickedly. 'I wonder what they've done?'

She dashed away gleefully from the stable. Anthony

sighed as he watched his sister go off. Here was yet another place where his family wasn't welcome. He hit his hand against the pony's stall in frustration, and Allegra suddenly became aware of her intrusion.

'I'm sorry. I'll go in.'

Anthony looked up as Allegra started out. He hurried to catch up with her. 'No, wait!'

Anthony had decided to go in with her. There was certainly no point to his staying out in the stables, and it was now a pleasure to both speak and be spoken to.

Anthony and Allegra entered the conservatory through the garden. Allegra lifted her heavy skirts delicately as she stepped into the room, while Anthony hurried in after, and threw himself in a chair. Anthony smiled.

'Ah! Sanctum, sanctorum!'

Allegra looked at Anthony as he lounged lazily in his chair.

'Won't the others talk to you then?'

Anthony seemed surprised, and a bit evasive. He finally answered, 'In their own way. But it's not easy being *persona non grata.*' He picked up the sketchbook which he'd left lying in the conservatory. He skimmed through a few pages, and then looked up at Allegra.

'Would you like to have a look at this?'

He held up a sketch for Allegra to see. Allegra moved, and sat beside Anthony, to study it. Her striking blue eyes became very serious.

'It's very different,' she began, gazing at it. 'And *good*,' she hastily finished.

Anthony laughed at her great politeness and looked at her good-naturedly. 'You're permitted to say if you don't like it!'

He turned over to one of the blank pages, and began sketching casually. Allegra spoke up more strongly.

'But I do!'

Anthony continued sketching, and pushed his blond hair out of his eyes. He used to be able to talk to Louisa like this, when she was younger. But he didn't seem to be able to now. She'd changed.

Allegra seemed a bit baffled, then answered, not unkindly. 'Louisa is very busy with her pony.'

Anthony shook his head while he continued to draw. 'No, she's not my little Poppet any more . . .'

He stopped sketching for a moment, and then shifted a bit so the light was better. He started sketching again with a sigh.

'Or perhaps it's me. I've done so many senseless things lately. Hurtful.'

'Like leaving the army?' Allegra asked curiously.

'No,' Anthony said softly. 'But I'll never court a Prince's lady friend again.' He gave a little laugh. 'Especially a Prince of Wales's.'

Allegra was now completely baffled. Her forehead wrinkled up as she spoke.

'I don't understand.'

Anthony stopped and looked up at the very young and the very confused Allegra. Despite her sophisticated clothes, her long brown hair and big blue eyes made her seem even younger than her sixteen years, and he was immediately ashamed. He answered very carefully and gently.

'No. Nor should you . . .'

Suddenly, coming from the hall, they heard the voice of Louisa, very loud and very upset.

'No! No, I won't!'

Anthony immediately looked up. What now?

And Anthony and Allegra were quickly on their feet, and hurrying towards the front hall.

In the hall Louisa, still in her riding habit, was arguing with Miss Craddock, who was unsuccessfully trying to get her up the stairs. Louisa stood at the bottom of the mahogany staircase and stamped her foot.

'It's not fair! Allegra's not having any more lessons!'

Miss Craddock tried to quieten Louisa down.

'She will,' her governess explained softly, 'just as soon as you've changed. And besides, you should have been back ages ago.' The girl had spent far too much time out riding on her pony.

Louisa struggled to make herself heard. She had had other things to do.

A door into the hallway opened, and Anthony came in. Allegra waited behind him in the doorway. He looked at his sister.

'What's all the fuss?'

Louisa was truly upset by now. Miss Craddock hadn't tried to understand her at all. She turned to her brother for justice.

'Anthony, Miss Craddock's being horrid!'

Miss Craddock quickly stepped forward. 'Now child, let's not bother Captain Anthony . . .'

Anthony looked at Louisa, annoyed. His peace had once again been disturbed. He spoke to her sharply. 'Come on child, off you go!'

Louisa's temper suddenly flared. Anthony hadn't even known what the matter was!

Anthony's anger rose to meet hers.

'I know you've been answering back a bit too much lately!'

Louisa looked stunned, as though she'd been slapped. She kept on talking, hoping Anthony would listen.

'Don't you even *care*? Why won't you ever listen to *me* any more? You always listen to *her*!'

Louisa glared at Allegra. Miss Craddock saw the look on Anthony's face, and tried to steer Louisa up the stairs. But Anthony turned to Louisa angrily. He couldn't bear being reprimanded.

'Louisa, your governess wants you! Do as you're told!'

Louisa took one last look at Anthony, then flew up the stairs, upset. She didn't stop running till she had reached her nursery door, which she closed with a bang.

* * *

Fran stood at the bottom of the staircase at Thornaby Hall, looking at some of the posters, and waiting. Allie rushed in, propelled by Shaun through the side entrance, but no sooner had Shaun got her through the door than he disappeared again,

Allie went to join her mother at the bottom of the stairs. She was suddenly aware of a quick burst of wind sweeping past her towards the stairs. Allie looked sharply around, but saw nothing there.

'My, you're jumpy today,' said Fran, greeting her daughter cheerfully. She looked towards the side exit. 'I suppose that's the last we'll see of Shaun.' They were all supposed to meet up here, after they had found Allie. She smiled at the thoughtful girl.

'Where did you go? Did you vanish into thin air?'

Allie started a bit, denying the possibility, and then quickly changed the subject. Had they found anything out yet?

'Not a sausage,' said Fran, reading another of the Water Board's posters. Allie spoke to her mother softly.

'Mum, do you believe in ghosts?'

Fran looked a bit surprised, then she laughed. 'Don't let Roger hear you say that! He'd disown you on the spot!'

She looked at Allie intently. 'But why darling? Don't tell me *you* do?'

Allie thought for a moment, and then dismissed it all. 'No, of course not,' she laughed.

Allie stared up at the empty staircase, and suddenly heard a distant door slam coming from one of the upper rooms. She turned to her mother but Fran had spotted

Roger and Shaun coming through the side door. She waved to them.

'Ah, here they come now.'

And Allie was left gazing up at the vacant staircase.

* * *

The next morning, Miss Craddock trudged up the staircase for the dozenth time, looking for Louisa. As she entered the nursery, she saw Louisa, still in her nightdress, standing at the washstand, slowly trickling some water from her jug into the bowl. Miss Craddock grew impatient. She hurried to Louisa.

'Oh Louisa, must I always stand over you? Everybody else had their breakfasts hours ago! And Allegra's been here for ages!'

Louisa reacted placidly, dipping her washcloth into the basin as she answered. She began to wash slowly. Not everyone could be like Allegra . . .

'No,' Miss Craddock answered kindly. 'But there are a few things you could learn from her.'

Miss Craddock watched as Louisa scrubbed lazily. She glanced at her watch. They were late enough as it was. Then Miss Craddock couldn't bear to see Louisa fiddling any longer. She took the washcloth herself, and helped her along.

'Oh child, do come along! Stop dawdling!'

Louisa grabbed the washcloth, and threw it back into the bowl, enraged. She was tired of receiving the wrong attention at the wrong times.

'I'm *not dawdling*!' Louisa screamed, and then turned away.

Allegra sat alone in her pretty new paisley frock in the conservatory, quietly reading her book. Anthony, dressed in his brown tweed riding habit and still wearing his cavalry boots, entered through the garden door. He greeted Allegra with a smile.

'Good morning!'

Allegra immediately got up, and gave Anthony a little curtsy.

'Louisa's not down yet, 'she explained quickly.

Anthony smiled. Louisa would probably be some time. Then he had a sudden thought. The horses were saddled. Would Allegra care for a ride?

Allegra at first seemed eager, but then her face fell. She thanked Anthony, but she wasn't terribly good with horses. It had never troubled her before.

'I could show you. You could have Turk. She's very gentle.'

Allegra shook her head politely. She didn't think Louisa would care for her riding her pony.

Anthony considered this for a moment, and then nodded. Picking up one of his sketchbooks, he went to sit in his favourite chair. He was feeling in a rather good humour.

'Do you ever draw?' he asked, looking up at Allegra.

Allegra once again shook her head. 'No. I'm worse at drawing than I am at ponies. Miss Craddock despairs.'

Anthony laughed, and then turned to one of his sketches. He showed it to Allegra.

'What do you think of that then?'

Allegra recognised the sketch with glee. It was his brothers, Thomas and Roderick.

'At an odd moment when they were standing still; yes,' Anthony admitted. 'But they're not as pretty as you!'

He studied Allegra's face quietly, almost professionally. It was a lovely face. Almost perfectly symmetrical. That was rare.

Anthony put his hand under Allegra's chin. She felt herself blushing as he talked.

'You have such a fine bone structure. And you're at such an interesting age. Another year or two and I wouldn't recognise you. And that would be such a pity.'

Allegra bowed her head, her cheeks reddening. Anthony realised she was shy and uncomfortable. He quickly withdrew his hand. He was sorry that he had embarrassed her. He showed her another sketch. It was another one of his brothers. Allegra spoke up shyly.

'It must be nice to have brothers.'

Anthony shrugged, and looked at her again. 'Don't you have any then?'

Allegra shook her head and explained. 'No, sisters. They're all married and live away. We hate not seeing them. My Mamma says she dreads when *I'll* go.'

Anthony suddenly brightened up, and scrambled to his feet. He'd had an idea. He started to pull a bewildered Allegra to her feet, laughing.

'Come on!' said Anthony as he pulled her by the hand.

'But why?' demanded Allegra as she started laughing too.

But Anthony wouldn't tell her. He just pulled Allegra through one of the open french doors, leading back into the library.

Louisa hurried down the stairs, Miss Craddock following closely behind her.

'Well then! I trust you girls are ready for your lessons?'

Louisa pushed past Mary, as the tweeny dusted the hall, and made her way towards the library door. She flew into the library just in time to see Anthony and Allegra, coming in through the french doors, laughing and talking, oblivious. Louisa quickly stepped back into the shadows, unnoticed. She watched in surprise, as Anthony joyously informed Allegra.

'It'll be a secret! *Our* secret!'

Louisa stared, terribly hurt and crushed.

* * *

Roger, Allie and Fran entered the church of St Swithin, chatting happily to the vicar. As they looked around they saw that the church of St Swithin had its pews covered in tarpaulins, and there were buckets of paint and the odd long ladder strewn all around. Roger was flummoxed.

'But I don't understand it! Whoever heard of a church being closed for Easter!'

The vicar smiled as they surveyed his half-painted church.

'We *are* still having services, Mr Burr. In our local church hall. But even Our Father's Mansion is sometimes in need of repair! Or so our plasterers tell me!' The long and lanky vicar looked at the Burrs and beamed.

Allie looked about the church distracted, not really taking it in. Roger continued with his questioning.

'But surely you must have some access to your records!'

The vicar turned his gaze to Roger. 'The most recent ones, of course. But you wouldn't be interested in last month's christenings?'

Roger shook his head sadly. No. The vicar sighed. He hadn't thought so. He folded his long fingers together, as if in prayer.

Fran tried to be helpful. 'But what about your older records? Where are they?'

'Stored away in our Mrs Pomerantz's attic.'

Roger quickly got his notebook and pen at the ready. 'And where is your Mrs Pomerantz?'

The vicar smiled. 'In Ibiza. On her annual holiday.'

Roger put his notebook away.

Fran tried again. Perhaps he could tell them something about Thornaby Hall itself.

The vicar pulled a thread from his jacket and thought. 'There's not a lot to tell really. The Water Board took it over in the early fifties.'

Roger was immediately interested. And before that?

The vicar put on his thinking cap again. 'It was used by

the Ministry For Food during the War. And before that, I believe it was a private hotel. And before that, Lord knows!' The vicar's hand flew to cover his mouth,

'Oh, I am sorry!'

Roger persevered.

'Might the name Hallam mean anything to you?'

The vicar immediately brightened. 'But of course!' He pushed his glasses back on his nose, and continued, his audience avid. '*Arthur* Hallam was a friend of the poet Tennyson!'

Roger interrupted eagerly. 'And *he* lived at Thornaby Hall, Rutland?'

The vicar shook his head. 'No, of course not. Nowhere near. Died in Italy I believe. Tennyson wrote a poem about it. 'In Memoriam'. I believe I have a copy somewhere. I'll get it!'

The vicar dashed away, leaving Roger open-mouthed and bewildered. Allie turned to her father, finally distracted and bored.

'Can't we go now?'

Roger rounded on her. '*You're* not paying much attention, Allie! You haven't asked a thing!' He would have expected it of Shaun, but he thought at least Allie would show willing.

Roger had a sudden thought, and then quickly looked about. Where *was* Shaun?

Fran looked at Roger. They had left him outside, swinging on a yew tree. Roger nodded, remembering. Allie edged towards the door.

The vicar came scurrying back, carrying a newspaper. He faced the Burrs eagerly.

'No, Mr Burr, I'm afraid you were right! Arthur Hallam was not one of our homegrown flowers. But I've found something else which might be of interest.'

He handed them a copy of their small local newspaper, *The Rutland Recorder*. Roger glanced at it as the vicar explained, 'It's been going quite a long time. It might be of some use!'

Fran looked over Roger's shoulder, and thanked the vicar for her husband.

The vicar beamed as he picked up a small tin. 'I'm glad I could help in some small way! Now—'. The vicar rattled the tin, and looked at the Burrs and smiled. 'Would you care to make a donation?'

Roger put his hand in his pocket.

Allie came out of the church and looked about. She saw its grey and barren graveyard, and various signs announcing the vicar's thoughts of the day and services, but she couldn't spot Shaun or anybody else.

She took a few deep breaths and was about to go back into the church when suddenly she saw Thornaby Hall in the distance. She stopped, and immensely curious, felt drawn in its direction.

* * *

Louisa hid behind a screen in the library, upset and shaken. Just inside the french doors she could see Anthony and Allegra, speaking softly and conspiratorially.

'What do you say Allegra? It would be so sporting!' Anthony was being his most persuasive, and charming. 'We could meet any time you like.'

Louisa watched, hurt, as Allegra's forehead crinkled in thought. But then Miss Craddock came into the library.

'Louisa! But where is Allegra? Why don't you call her?'

Miss Craddock then spotted Allegra coming in through the french doors with Anthony. Allegra was happy and animated, her eyes shining. She apologised immediately.

'Oh, I'm sorry, Miss Craddock; were you looking for me?'

Anthony smiled at the governess charmingly. 'All my

fault. I've kept her too long. I'll let you get on with your lessons.'

He began to withdraw from the room. Louisa sprang forward, anxious to speak to him. She hadn't meant to be silly yesterday . . .

Anthony turned to his sister absently. 'Not to worry, Poppet.' He hadn't given it a second thought.

He smiled at Louisa and Allegra, as he made his way happily from the room. And Louisa fumed as she watched Allegra return the smile.

Later that afternoon, Miss Craddock escorted the two girls down the stairs. They were dressed for sport, wearing some of their older and plainer frocks, which Allegra detested. Louisa carried a rubber ball, and seemed pale and subdued. Miss Craddock lectured them kindly.

'A spot of rounders will do you the world of good! You've been looking a bit peaky this afternoon, Louisa!'

Louisa didn't answer, and Miss Craddock looked at her charge, concerned. She decided that perhaps Louisa was still a little bit out of sorts from that morning. Or was coming down with a chill. Miss Craddock decided to fetch another shawl. She stopped, and addressed her charges.

'Wait here for a moment, girls!'

She disappeared back up the stairs, and Louisa relaxed and fingered the rounders ball.

'Oh I do like rounders!' said Allegra happily.

Louisa stopped and looked at Allegra. Was that her game? Louisa looked out at her from under her long lashes. 'Yes, rounders can be awfully sporting, like so many other things – and people – don't you think?'

Louisa started to fidget and fan herself as Allegra looked at her, surprised. Louisa pushed her long dark brown hair out of her face, and tried to loosen her collar. She seemed paler. Allegra was concerned.

'Are you all right?'

Louisa faltered a bit, uncertain. 'Oh yes, I think so. It's just so fusty in here; so musty. I feel faint . . .'

Allegra immediately turned on her heel. 'I'll go and get Miss Craddock!'

But Louisa had grabbed her before she could move a step.

'No, Allegra, don't leave me!'

And she began to swoon.

* * *

Allie had arrived at Thornaby Hall, and finding the outside car-park empty, went into the front hall. The place looked deserted, as all the Water Board workers had gone home for the day. The Hall was silent. She decided to look about.

* * *

Shaking on the staircase, Louisa desperately clutched at the banister, Allegra trying to help her. She cried out to Allegra, she was so dizzy, and so hot—

Allegra grabbed for Louisa's hand.

'Then please sit down!'

Louisa put her hand out, but as she did so, she dropped the rubber ball. It bounced down the stairs.

* * *

Allie was looking about the maps in the front hall, when suddenly she heard something bouncing down the staircase. She spun quickly round to have a look, but she saw nothing there. Allie tried to have a closer look.

* * *

Louisa held on to Allegra unsteadily and desperately, trying to regain her balance. Allegra also tried to grasp the banister for support.

'Louisa, please let me hold onto the banister!'

But just as Louisa was about to sit down, she stumbled forward, knocking Allegra, and causing the girl to lose her balance. Allegra began to fall forward.

'Oh help!'

Allegra started to fall down the stairs, terrified, when suddenly she was caught from behind and forcibly pulled backwards by Miss Craddock. Louisa watched in horror.

'Girls! What are you doing?' Miss Craddock's voice shook as she tried to comfort Allegra.

Allegra did her best to speak. 'Louisa was ill . . .'

But before Allegra could finish her sentence, Louisa collapsed unconscious, in a faint. Miss Craddock flew to her side.

'Oh my goodness! *Louisa*!'

* * *

Allie was still peering round on the stairs when suddenly she heard,

'Louisa! *Louisa*!'

She spun round to see where the faint voice came from, but only spotted Fran, who had obviously been standing there for quite some minutes. Fran stood looking at her watch, evidentally not noticing a thing that had happened. Allie was startled but relieved as she joined her mother at the bottom of the stairs. Fran smiled at her daughter.

'Where were you? We were wondering what you've been up to!'

Allie answered, thinking quickly. She had just wanted some air.

Fran agreed, sympathising entirely. 'Yes, that church was rather close.'

Fran noticed Allie gazing up the staircase again. She

didn't look at all well. Fran went to her side.

'Darling, are you all right?'

Allie recovered quickly. 'Yes, of course.'

Fran looked at her, a bit worried, and persisted, 'Are you sure?'

Allie stared up at her mother, desperately wanting to confide in her. But at the last minute, her fears and reason got the better of her. Allie musn't be silly!

'Of course! Allie repeated, heading quickly for the door. 'Let's go!'

She flew out of the side exit, Fran chasing after her.

* * *

Allegra waited in the front hall for the carriage, her hat and coat resting neatly in her lap. Anthony passed through from the study, and saw her. He went up to her, surprised.

'Are you going already?'

Allegra explained quietly that she was being sent home early. 'I don't think Louisa is at all well. Miss Craddock thought she should lie down.'

Anthony was immediately concerned. He'd look in on Louisa later. But first he spoke to Allegra again. 'Must you dash straight off?'

Allegra lowered her gaze. 'My Fraulein will be here soon. I'm expected.'

Anthony heard the sound of a carriage and pair outside. He helped Allegra on with her coat. They would meet tomorrow.

Allegra nodded as Anthony opened the door, and escorted her out to her carriage. The door was left ajar, which caused a breeze which blew onto Louisa, who was hiding by the top of the staircase.

When Anthony and Allegra had gone out of the door, Louisa started to sneak down the stairs, their conversation and her long skirt weighing down every step. She gathered her skirts and came carefully down. But she had not yet reached the front door when Anthony strolled back in.

'Louisa!' he exclaimed in surprise. 'I thought you were not well!'

Louisa avoided his question, and headed for the open door.

'I've got to tend to Turk.'

'I'll see to that! You go back upstairs.' Anthony put out a hand to stop her, and let it rest on his sister's shoulder fondly. Louisa shook it off, breaking away.

'No!' she cried, beginning to dash out, 'Turk's expecting *me*!' And she ran through the open front door and out before Anthony could stop her.

The stable was dark and forlorn as Louisa huddled against Turk, her chestnut pony nuzzling up to her. She hugged her pony.

'They're being beastly Turk, *beastly*.'

She buried her face in the pony's side. She confided in her further. 'And I know it's all Allegra's fault. But I don't mind. Because we'll have our own secret. Because I'm going to let Allegra ride you tomorrow.'

Louisa moved from her pony, her only friend, and went to where some tools were hanging on a shelf. She thought for a moment, and then desperate and unhappy, Louisa selected an awl and set to work on the strap on the pony's side-saddle.

* * *

4
The Ride

Roger and Shaun were attempting to cook on a camping stove as Allie and Fran arrived back from the Hall. Tins littered the table as Roger slaved away over a hot stove. He gave Allie a quick glance as she came in.

'Allie, where did you get to?'

Allie shivered, trying to get warm, as she huddled near the hot cooker.

Shaun studied his sister as she gazed off into the stove's small fire.

'Allie, are you all right? You look terrible!'

Allie started, and lifted her head, amazed at Shaun's concern, and perception. But before she could answer, he was his usual self.

'But then again, so does Fran!'

Shaun moved quickly as Fran took a cursory swipe at him. Roger announced dinner.

'This is fit for a king! Grab a pew!'

The dinner consisted of mince, which was overcooked. It went well with the potatoes which were hardly cooked at all. Roger put a lump of the meal on Fran's plate. She looked at it.

'Well, today's been a complete failure.'

Roger looked at his wife in despair. Now how could she say that? He conceded that they were no further ahead than yesterday, but then perhaps they would have made more progress if a certain member of the family hadn't kept on disappearing!

He pointedly handed a plate to Allie. She took it, without looking at him or it. Fran helped Shaun to some food.

'So what's on the agenda for tomorrow?'

Roger put down the serving spoon promptly. 'I'm glad you asked. Newspapers!'

The family groaned.

'I've been looking through the local newspaper from the vicar and I think it would be time well spent to pay them a visit! To see if we can't learn anything about Thornaby Hall or the Hallams, from their files! After all, our work must continue!'

The family now all moaned louder. Roger at first put it down to the food. But Shaun soon spoke up.

'Can't we give it a rest?'

Roger looked at his young son, horrified. Fran quickly joined in.

'You do realise that this is supposed to be their holiday. And they haven't had any real fun!'

Allie looked up from the table, her blue eyes troubled. Suddenly the holiday didn't seem like fun to her. She was frightened. And she couldn't reason *why*.

'Is it all so very important to you?'

Roger looked at Allie, surprised that she had spoken out. Allie was surprised too. Roger turned to his family in all seriousness.

'Do I sense a mutiny?'

The family nodded their heads as Roger looked on in despair. They were preparing the plank now.

He looked from face to face, and then came to a conclusion. 'Look, we'll strike a bargain. We'll give it one last try. And if we come a cropper this time, I'll work alone, and we'll retreat to a proper hotel. I promise!'

Roger sat down at the table, picked up his fork, and began to eat the supper he had prepared. After one bite, he choked. The family laughed, at last satisfied.

Allie huddled round the cottage's small, cracked sink, trying to clean her teeth, as her father trailed about with a newspaper, *The Rutland Recorder*.

Roger dipped the newspaper in Allie's water as he read out: 'Established 1860! That ought to serve our purpose!'

Allie moved to get away from Roger, and he promptly moved along with her.

'Oh show some interest, Allie!'

Allie rinsed her mouth, and turned to her father. 'How far back do the Hallams go?'

'I'm not sure.' Roger leafed through his newspaper again. Allie dried her hands, persisting.

'But why are you so interested in them? Why should you care who they were?'

Roger looked up. 'Why not? It's interesting.'

It was Allie's turn to follow Roger as he moved from the sink.

'But isn't it an invasion? Don't you feel you might be disturbing things?'

Roger turned to his daughter in amazement.

'What are you talking about?' He wondered if she had seen too many horror films back in London. He put down his paper. 'It's an historian's *job* to find out who they were! Families like the Hallams are of enormous interest to people like us today! It's only by understanding the past that we have any hope of coping with our present!'

He sat down heavily at the table and started to go through his notes. Allie took all her courage in her hands, and went to her father.

'Dad, can I ask you something?'

Roger was busy flipping through his papers. 'Anything!'

'Are there any such things as ghosts?'

Roger stopped what he was doing, and looked up at his daughter in surprise. She was looking at him intently.

'What put that into your head?'

Allie shrugged. 'Don't ghosts exist then?'

Roger was adamant. 'Of course they do!'

Allie was surprised and relieved. She had started to feel warm and safe. Roger continued.

'In primitive societies, which also believe in black magic, spirit-worship and sacrifices; human and goat!'

Allie's heart sank but she carried on. 'But what about all the civilised people who claim they've seen ghosts?'

Roger nodded emphatically. 'There's a technical term for them.'

Allie leaned forward eagerly. 'What?'

'Nutters!' Roger looked at his daughter very carefully. He wished Fran was about. 'Allie, you haven't met any superstitious locals, have you?'

Allie shook her head under Roger's watchful stare, and suddenly felt ashamed. He persisted.

'Have you heard about anything? Or thought you'd seen something when you've been off on your own?'

Roger stood up, and Allie faced her father. For a moment, she was torn. She desperately wanted his comfort and reassurance, but she also needed his respect. Why did he always need *facts*?

The door to the cottage flew open, and Fran bounded in.

Roger looked at Allie, and Allie at Roger. But the moment was lost. Allie merely shook her head, and turned quickly away. Roger seemed relieved.

'Good! Because there are enough cranks in the world as it is! And besides, you're your father's daughter, aren't you?' He gave Allie a little hug.

'Now I want everyone to bed! It's late enough as it is! I'll fetch Shaun!'

Roger released Allie. 'Now, bed!'

* * *

Louisa was still working on the pony's saddle when she heard Miss Craddock calling her in the distance. She paused for a moment and listened.

'Louisa, Louisa. Where are you?'

She hastily finished with the saddle, and returned the

tools to their proper place. Miss Craddock went on calling, and Louisa blew out the single candle in the stable as the governess drew near.

She tried to keep still and small as a light flickered outside the stable window. The light threw shadows which danced on the walls. The light passed, and Louisa sighed in relief but no sooner had it gone than the stable door began to open, silently and swiftly, giving Louisa no time to catch her breath. Miss Craddock slid into the stables.

'Louisa! But what are you doing out here in the dark?'

Louisa scrambled to her feet, and explained that she was tending to Turk. But Miss Craddock was not pleased.

'You must come into the house at once! You have not been well!'

Miss Craddock clucked over her as she escorted Louisa from the stable. Louisa went quietly, almost happily, but took one last glance at the pony's girth as they departed.

Miss Craddock tucked Louisa snugly into the warmth of her waiting bed. She felt Louisa's hand.

'Silly girl, you are frozen! Like ice! You'll be ill!'

Louisa huddled her feet close to the comforting stone hot-water bottle resting at the edge of her bed. She sighed, 'Miss Craddock. Do you think Allegra might like to ride my pony tomorrow?'

Miss Craddock was trying to settle Louisa down. She spoke softly. 'I'm sure I don't know about that!'

Louisa tried to sit up but Miss Craddock stopped her.

'But I'd like her to.'

Miss Craddock nodded soothingly to Louisa as she smoothed her blankets for the night.

'Fine. But tomorrow. Now sleep!'

Louisa smiled as Miss Craddock turned down the gaslight.

* * *

The Burr family slept in their respective beds in the small, ramshackle one-roomed cottage. Vague nocturnal noises could be heard from outside; owls hooting, cats calling, trees rustling.

They all slept peacefully, except for Allie, who tossed and turned on her hard camp bed. She cried out softly as she dreamed, of the muted door slam that she heard her first time in Thornaby Hall. Of the gust of wind, which passed her by; the bouncing ball she could not see; the haunting laugh outside the empty stable. They all joined together in one nightmarish dream, till the sound of that laughter grew louder and louder, and Allie could once again hear the girl's name being called in the Hall.

'Louisa! *Louisa*!'

She sat bolt upright in her bed.

'Louisa!'

Then suddenly she woke. And looking quickly around, Allie found herself amongst the fast-asleep Burrs, frightened.

With a sigh and a shiver, Allie sank back down into her pillow, and closed her eyes, listening to Roger's snoring.

The next morning was bright and sunny as Fran, already dressed, bent over the still sleeping Allie.

'Rise and shine, Sleepyhead!'

Allie woke with a start, and was at first disorientated. She focused groggily on Fran.

'Come on and greet the new day!'

Allie looked round to see the rest of the Burrs already dressed and circulating. Shaun was munching a piece of toast.

'We let you sleep. You were zonked!'

Shaun dropped the crumbs from his toast over Allie's bed. Roger also bounded over.

'As soon as you've dressed and eaten, it's us for the newspapers! An historian never rests!'

Allie finally found her voice. 'No!'

Roger registered surprise and turned to Fran.

She perched herself on Allie's bed and felt Allie's forehead.

'What's the matter, darling? Aren't you well?'

Allie nodded from where she lay in her bed. She felt fine.

Fran worried as she looked at her daughter. She didn't feel feverish, but she had been looking a bit peaky lately. Fran made her decision.

'I think I'd better stay with you.'

Allie sat up in her bed. 'No, honestly, I'm all right. All I want is a bit of rest!'

Allie looked pleadingly at her mother. Fran was unconvinced, but got up anyway.

Fran and Roger and Shaun pulled on their coats; Shaun now wishing he'd thought of Allie's idea first. As they prepared to leave, Fran turned back.

'You take care now.'

The moment that they were gone, Allie sprang from her bed, and grabbed some clothes. She hastily dressed, and then quickly left the cottage.

* * *

Anthony came into Louisa's nursery to wish her good morning, but he was almost bowled over by Louisa who was rushing out of her room. She was dressed in her new riding habit, and was trying to adjust her top hat and veil as she ran into her brother. Anthony steadied himself and Louisa, and laughed. 'What's the rush?'

Louisa looked up at Anthony, happy and exuberant.

'I'm going riding!'

He smiled good-naturedly.

'I'm going to let Allegra ride too!'

Louisa looked up at Anthony and beamed, and then broke away, and made a dash for the stairs, eager to get out.

Anthony looked on in surprise, and quickly called after her.

'That was very kind!'

But Louisa was already out of sight.

Louisa came racing down the stairs just as Allegra was handing her hat and coat and gloves to Finch, the butler. She descended upon her and seized her.

'Come Allegra! You're going riding with me!'

Allegra was rather taken aback, and couldn't think of anything she'd like less. She answered politely that she wasn't very good with ponies.

Louisa paid her no heed.

'Nonsense, nothing could be easier! And I'll even let you ride Turk!'

Allegra was still dubious, having not brought her riding habit. Louisa was unperturbed. She would loan Allegra one of hers.

She grabbed Allegra, and started pulling her up the stairs. Allegra tried one last protest. Miss Craddock would be wanting them soon!

Louisa was not going to let such a little thing as that stand in her way. She told Allegra finally and firmly, 'We won't be long! Don't be such a rabbit!'

And she pulled Allegra the rest of the way up the stairs.

When Louisa and Allegra came back into the hall, they were both wearing riding habits. Allegra's was grey, and not as well fitting as Louisa's black, and she fussed with it to get it right, before anyone could see her. But before Louisa could whisk her out of the door, Anthony came down the stairs carrying his sketching pad. He stopped when he saw the girls.

'Ah, Allegra. Just the person I wanted to see!'

Louisa grabbed Allegra's arm.

'She's coming with me!'

Anthony watched in surprise as Allegra was dragged off

by the adamant Louisa. Miss Craddock then emerged from the schoolroom, looking, as usual, for her charge. She addressed Anthony with a sigh.

'Now where did Louisa go?'

Anthony shrugged. 'Off for a ride with Allegra.'

Miss Craddock looked at Anthony in surprise. 'Allegra?'

Anthony nodded and laughed, and headed out the front door with his sketching pad.

Louisa and Allegra had emerged from the house and started straight towards the stables. It was a clear, bright day, and Louisa looked happily at the acres of green, open paddock that she loved to ride in. The girls were progressing awkwardly in their riding skirts when a rugby ball suddenly flew their way. It was followed by Thomas, Louisa's fourteen-year-old brother.

Brothers were supposed to look alike, but Thomas was nothing like Anthony, Louisa thought bitterly as the boy ran to collect his ball.

He was as chubby as Anthony was lean; as dark as Anthony was blond and blue-eyed; and as clumsy as Anthony was graceful. Louisa had never had all that much to do with Thomas, or with her seventeen-year-old brother Roderick either, for that matter, because the girls had always been kept separately in the nursery with their governess, while the boys were sent off properly to public school.

But she had seen enough to know that she had never liked Thomas very much. He was such a tease.

Thomas pushed his long brown hair out of his eyes, and addressed the two girls.

'Hello! Going for a ride!'

Allegra nodded shyly as Louisa tried to steer them past. But Thomas quickly attached himself to them.

'Can I have a go too?'

Louisa turned and faced her podgy brother, who was

waiting hopefully. Why did he have to come now?

'No! This ride is for *Allegra*!'

And Louisa pulled Allegra off towards the open paddock, which was ablaze with wild flowers. Thomas followed them.

* * *

Allie had strolled to Thornaby Hall, and now stood outside, by the Water Board's car park, looking up at it, strangely drawn. She studied the house curiously, and then turned and headed out across the Hall's open paddock.

* * *

Anthony came out of Thornaby Hall with his sketchbook and watched the three children, his brother and sister and Allegra, quickly crossing the paddock. He smiled as he set off himself, towards the copse where he could happily sit and sketch.

The groom had brought the ponies out to the paddock. Turk was standing quietly and patiently, her side-saddle firmly in place. The chestnut pony nuzzled Louisa as she came near. But Allegra still looked at the pony with reluctance.

'Oh come, Louisa, Allegra doesn't even *want* to ride!'

Louisa ignored Thomas as she prepared to help Allegra mount. 'Would you like some help up?'

Thomas quickly pushed past them, and bounded up onto the pony.

'All right!'

And before Louisa or Allegra could do anything, Thomas had dug his heels into the pony, and had taken off across the paddock. Louisa stood there screaming.

'Thomas! *No*!'

But Thomas raced across the paddock on Turk, laughing

happily as he went. Too happy to notice that the saddle's girth was starting to give way beneath him.

He headed out across the paddock viewed by Anthony, who was watching while he sketched.

Thomas had steered Turk out near some trees and was about to attempt a jump over a felled log. But just as the pony and the boy were leaving the ground, the saddle's girth snapped, and the pony stumbled, pitching her rider over her head into some bracken. Then Turk fell too.

Louisa watched in anguish as Anthony, throwing aside his sketchbook, and then she and Allegra raced towards the scene of the accident.

Anthony reached there first.

'Thomas! Are you hurt?'

He flew to his brother, who was scrambling to his feet, dirty and shaken. The pony was lying very still on the ground, unable to get up. Thomas straightened up. He was fine.

Anthony glared at him, and then turned his attention to the pony. He examined the little horse very carefully and gently, then he turned to Thomas.

'This pony's not all right.'

'The saddle just snapped beneath me!' Thomas watched his brother as he tended to the pony. Anthony threw him a look.

'I'll deal with you later.'

Allegra and Louisa caught up with the Hallam brothers, and Louisa quickly knelt beside Anthony, frightened and worried. She cradled Turk's head in her arms.

'She'll be all right —' Louisa looked at Anthony. 'Won't she?'

Anthony stood up, and avoided looking at his sister.

'Allegra, why don't you take Louisa back into the house?'

Louisa looked at her brother and cried. She stroked her horse lightly.

Anthony took Louisa gently by the arm, and helped her to her feet. He looked at her kindly. 'Poppet, please go inside.'

He put his arm around Louisa, and at the same time, gave a quick nod to Thomas. Thomas understood, and dashed hastily back towards the Hall. Louisa saw and slowly began to comprehend.

'No!' she screamed as she watched Thomas race away.

Anthony spoke as kindly and as gently as possible.

'Louisa, the pony's leg is broken.'

Louisa tried to shake off Anthony's arm. 'It couldn't be!'

Anthony held her. 'Poppet, the pony is suffering!' Anthony turned to Allegra and ordered, 'Allegra, take her in!'

Louisa broke away, hysterical and tormented. 'No!' she screamed, as Allegra moved to take her away.

* * *

Allie wandered in the paddock, enjoying the quiet, near some trees. Some wild flowers grew out of a felled log, and she reached her hand out and smiled. She was about to pick a flower when suddenly she heard a sharp, ringing rifle shot. She spun round but saw no one. Another rifle shot rang out. She threw her hands over her ears in horror, forgetting the flower.

'No!!'

And Allie ran away from the paddock, stumbling and crying.

* * *

Allegra stood alone in the front hall by the door, when Anthony burst in, concerned and agitated.

'Where's Louisa?'

She pointed towards the polished staircase, and Anthony

saw a very small and very agonised Louisa, huddled on a stair, crying. He went up to her, and spoke to her softly.

'Louisa.'

Anthony reached out a hand to comfort her, but Louisa recoiled in horror.

'Leave me alone!'

Anthony sat down beside Louisa and put an arm around her.

'Poppet, I'm sorry about what happened. But accidents do happen —'

Louisa broke away, distraught. 'Accident! But it wasn't an accident!'

Anthony tried to quieten his crying sister, but she wouldn't let him. She was beyond all reason.

'It's all your fault! You killed my pony!'

Louisa hit out at Anthony, and Anthony let her.

'You shot her! You shot my pony!'

Anthony tried to be gentle. 'Now don't be silly . . .'

Allegra moved forward. There had been no choice.

Louisa looked at Allegra, and suddenly her sorrow turned to hatred. 'And I hate you too!'

Louisa scrambled to her feet, enraged. She turned to include Anthony. 'I'll never forgive any of you! *Never*!'

She ran sobbing up the stairs, as Anthony watched sadly from the hallway.

* * *

Allie ran into the empty cottage, breathless. She slammed the door behind her, tears streaming down her face. She threw herself onto her bed, and sobbed her heart out, frightened.

Roger, Fran and Shaun were wading through heaps of files in the *Rutland Recorder*'s information office. The office was little more than a cupboard with filing cabinets, papers and dust but Roger scanned the papers as carefully as if he had been at the British Museum. He got up to collect yet another assortment of files. Shaun wiped his hands on his jumper.

'Was this journey really necessary?'

'Yes!' growled Roger as he passed. Fran turned to their son a little more kindly.

'What's the matter? Getting tired?'

Shaun shook his head. Bored. They had been there all morning, and he had had more than enough.

'I was just thinking. About Allie,' continued Fran, 'don't you think it would be a good idea if one of us went back, and had a look at her?'

Almost before Fran had got her last word out, Shaun was up, and racing towards the door. He didn't need prompting twice.

He ran into Roger, who was carrying in yet another load of files. He was free!

Roger lost his hold on the files, and dozens of files, clippings and papers scattered to the four corners.

'Hey!'

But it was too late. Shaun was gone. Roger knelt and started picking up his papers from the floor. Some had footprints. Roger looked up and called after Shaun.

'Slacker!'

Fran and Roger were still wading through the piles and piles of papers, but they were becoming more and more disheartened. Fran skimmed through some of the files before her.

'Hallam . . . Hallam . . . there just aren't any Hallams!'

Roger picked up another file, and blew the dust off. He choked. 'Try a little later.'

Fran glanced at the files in front of her, and looked at the dates. 'I'm already up to 1870! And I'm not sure if that's the year, or the number of files we've looked through!'

Roger ploughed on at his task. Fran was becoming exasperated.

'Roger, just what are you hoping to find?'

Roger put down his files, and turned to his wife. By now, he was trying to convince himself as well as Fran.

'Surely something somewhere must have been written about the Hallam family! One of Rutland's major families couldn't just disappear, without leaving a record or a trace. It goes against the historical grain!'

Fran spoke up quietly from her corner. 'I don't know if it's the same family, but I've just found a Hallam.'

Fran had never seen Roger move so fast, except at mealtimes. 'Who is it? What's it about?'

Fran studied the file, which wasn't easy with Roger peering over her shoulder. She couldn't be sure.

'I don't know. But it's something about a "Captain Anthony Hallam".'

Roger quickly grabbed the file.

* * *

Anthony stood outside Louisa's nursery door, trying to turn the handle. The door was locked. He called inside.

'Louisa! Won't you open the door?'

There was no reply, as Louisa sat inside her bedroom, white and tightlipped.

Anthony rattled the knob again. He tried a second time.

'Poppet, it's me!'

Louisa wouldn't even budge. Anthony was becoming aggravated. 'Louisa, won't you even listen?!'

He grew steadily angrier. He banged against the door.

'Did you hear me? I said open this door!'

There was still no reply. With a shrug of his shoulders he turned and headed down the stairs, making for the front door. Miss Craddock came out from the study and stopped him. She was obviously upset.

'Captain Anthony, where are you going?'

He stopped short, and looked at her coldly.

'I beg your pardon?'

Miss Craddock came to him nervously, realising her mistake, and spoke to him more gently.

'I'm sorry. It's just that your Papa wishes to speak to you.'

Anthony headed for the front door, having heard all he wanted to of children and ponies for one day. Miss Craddock stepped anxiously towards him.

'I believe it's *not* about the accident.'

Anthony stopped again, waiting for Miss Craddock to continue.

'Some tradesmen came to call on him. About the opening of some accounts. I think your father's terribly angry. What should I tell him?'

Anthony turned and faced her. She was after all but a messenger. And a kind one. He changed course and stormed straight for the study, annoyed.

'Oh, I'll tell him myself!'

As Anthony thundered into the study angrily, Miss Craddock quickly hurried away.

Louisa came down the stairs, clutching an old doll to her tightly. Her dark hair was in disarray, and her eyes were red from her tears. She stepped silently into the hall, and then noticed a light shining from the schoolroom. The door was ajar, and she crept up to peek in. She saw Allegra gathering up some books.

'What are *you* doing here?'

Louisa glared as she watched Allegra putting the books into a red velvet bag. Allegra hesitated, then tried to explain.

'My parents have sent me to collect my things.'

She looked at Louisa's taut white face, and added quickly that her Fraulein was waiting outside for her.

Louisa stood in the doorway, blocking Allegra. She had

only heard one thing. 'Collect your things? Why?'

Allegra looked up at Louisa with those big blue eyes that Louisa had come to despise. 'Because I'm going away. To London. For the season. My family's decided I should join them in London. They'll be getting someone to teach me there.'

Louisa felt her spirits rising for the first time.

'So I won't be having lessons with you any longer. I'll be leaving tomorrow.' Allegra added tentatively. 'I hope you won't mind.'

'No, of course not!' Louisa was delighted. She hugged her doll closer. She smiled as Allegra started to say goodbye, but then cut her short, and held her hand out. Allegra took it, surprised.

'Good-bye.'

Louisa waited until Allegra had gone, and then she clapped her hands in glee and laughed.

Anthony came out of the study, rather shaken and angry. He stopped when he saw Louisa at the hall window, gleefully looking out onto the drive. She turned and called to him.

'Anthony!'

He joined her at the window. 'I thought you weren't speaking to me.' Anthony fumbled inside his jacket pocket for his cigarette case.

Louisa looked up at him, her green eyes sparkling. 'Allegra's gone!'

Anthony found a cigarette, and lit it. 'Yes, so I've heard.'

Louisa grabbed Anthony's hand, and hung onto it happily.

'Isn't that lovely? Won't it be much much better at the Hall without her?'

Anthony withdrew his hand and turned away sharply, taking long angry puffs on his cigarette.

'The Hall be hanged! I shan't be staying here any longer!

It's time I was able to lead my own life again, in my own way. So I'll be going up to London. Tomorrow!'

Anthony stormed off towards the library leaving Louisa stunned and dismayed.

* * *

Shaun rushed into the rickety cottage, licking an ice-cream cone he had bought along the way.

'Allie, I'm home!' Shaun had second thoughts. 'Not that I would call this home!'

He looked up from his ice-cream to see Allie huddled on her bed. She'd been crying. Concerned, Shaun hurried over to her.

'Allie, are you sick? Have you been hurt?'

She just shook her head, unable to speak. Shaun was getting worried. 'Then what's the matter?'

Allie found her voice. 'It's nothing.'

Shaun had never seen Allie like this. She rarely cried.

'Allie, it can't be nothing! Go on, you can tell me. *Please*. Something is wrong, isn't it? Allie what is it?'

Allie turned and collapsed in tears on the shaky camp bed. She blurted out, 'Shaun, I can't tell you!'

How could she tell her brother she'd been experiencing ghosts?

5

The Trip

'Allie, something's happening, isn't it?'

Allie looked up at her brother, and for the first time saw someone she might be able to confide in. She had to speak to someone, or crack up. She said hesitantly.

'I've been *feeling* things; experiencing them. At the Hall.'

Shaun stared at his sister in shock. He wasn't quite sure what she was trying to tell him, but he hoped it wasn't what he thought.

'Allie, have you seen a ghost?'

Allie heard Shaun's words and totally broke down.

'No, I haven't *seen* one. But I can *feel* one and *hear* one. I can feel a pull on me!'

Shaun had heard enough. He quickly straightened up and headed for the door. This was a job for Fran and Roger. Allie pleaded with him, 'Shaun, no! They won't understand! It can't be happening!'

Shaun took one last look at his sister, then quickly hurried out the door. He wouldn't be long. A chap had to do what he thought best.

He left Allie sobbing on the camp bed.

* * *

Louisa tried desperately not to cry as she rattled the doorknob of the library door. She *had* to speak to Anthony; she had to get all this straightened out. If only Anthony would open the library door . . .

Louisa did not hear the swish of Miss Craddock's skirts as the governess came up behind her.

'Louisa! You ought to be in bed!'

Louisa went on shaking the doorknob as Miss Craddock

tried to lead her gently away. Louisa had only one thing on her mind.

'Allegra is going away.'

Miss Craddock looked rather surprised, and she faced her charge. 'Yes, Allegra is going to London. But how did you know?'

Louisa was too upset to answer coherently. Her voice shook as she spoke. 'It's all my fault. I didn't mean it to happen! I've been horrid to Anthony!'

Miss Craddock began to worry that the pony's death had upset Louisa even more than she had thought. The child was so like her mother. The best place for her would be bed. She tried to guide Louisa gently.

'Come now, you've had a nasty shock.'

Louisa resisted. She tried to explain.

'I made them all go!'

She looked up at Miss Craddock's kind and gentle face. It was the face she had seen as long as she could remember; a comforting face, a reassuring face, which had been there whenever she needed. And she never needed her more than now. She begged Miss Craddock. 'Please help me!'

Miss Craddock looked down on her with surprise. 'What are you talking about, child? What could *you* possibly have done?'

She saw that the girl was shivering, and instinctively took off her own shawl and put it around Louisa's shoulders. She waited as Louisa seemed about to speak, then they suddenly heard a movement coming from within the library itself. It was Anthony. No sooner had she heard that than Louisa had broken away from Miss Craddock.

She shook the handle of the library door once more. 'Anthony please let me in!'

And the library door opened.

* * *

Fran tried to peer over Roger's shoulder as he hogged the Anthony Hallam file for himself. But she was the first to spot what they were looking for.

'Ah, here it is,' she said, giving Roger a push, 'Anthony Hallam, Captain. Commissioned Spring 1870; Cavalry, 13th Hussars. Served York, Sheffield, Chatham, Hamilton . . . and India!'

Roger jostled for a better position as Fran now took over the file. They had still not quite found what he had wanted. He answered impatiently, 'Very interesting. But is he any relation to the Thornaby Hallams?'

Fran continued to skim through the material, and came across another yellowed piece of paper. 'Eldest son of Sir *Reginald* Hallam . . .'

Roger once again shook his head. It didn't ring a bell. Fran went on with her reading.

'Late of Thornaby Hall, Rutland!' Fran looked up at Roger triumphantly. 'We found it!' But Fran's face suddenly clouded over as she read on. Roger grabbed back the file to see what had perplexed his wife. His face also took on a puzzled look.

'For further information, see 1875, Indian tour, His Royal Highness, Edward, Prince of Wales . . .'

And Roger carefully placed the Anthony Hallam file to one side, and attacked the filing cabinet again.

* * *

Louisa burst into the library just in time to see Anthony collecting his papers from the large oak desk, and then move on to fill his cigarette case from a box on the table. His movements were stiff and jerky, like a man tempted to throw the whole lot out of the window, but not daring. He didn't look up as Louisa spoke.

'Please Anthony, what are you doing? Can't we talk?'

Anthony closed his cigarette case, and started for the

library door. Louisa was suddenly frightened, but still she blocked his way.

'But you mustn't go! You can't leave me!'

Anthony stopped abruptly, and looked down at his sister. He saw her large green eyes pleading up at him, her face still tear-stained. He had always hated to see her unhappy. He answered her softly, 'But why must I stay?'

He looked at Louisa, and wished he could spare her this, but felt he had to explain.

'I'm sorry, Louisa, but I can't hang fire any longer. I don't belong with the family; I've been treated as a child, and I'm a man; a soldier. Used to standing on my own. But I'm not out to hurt you Poppet.'

Anthony stroked his sister's face gently. She felt she was winning. Louisa looked up at him, eagerly. 'Then take me with you!'

Anthony looked surprised. 'That's out of the question!'

Louisa tried to control the rage that she felt boiling up within her. 'But Allegra's going to London!'

Anthony was honestly surprised. 'Is she?'

'Soon! Don't say you didn't know!'

Anthony looked at the trembling Louisa and wished he were back with his regiment, where everything was so orderly. There was no need for explanations there.

'Louisa, I've got to start living *my* life again! I just can't go on paying for something I don't consider important! I have to start thinking of myself again! And what *I* want to do!'

Louisa didn't believe a word he'd said, and threw her hands over her ears, enraged. Anthony made one last attempt to reach her.

'Louisa, can't you understand?'

Then he stormed out of the room, eager to be gone.

* * *

Allie sat where Shaun had left her, turning things over and over again in her mind. This couldn't be happening. What was it? Allie spoke, as if someone was in the room.

'Oh Louisa, who are you?'

But all she heard was the gurgling of the cottage's rusty pipes. Suddenly Allie decided that this thing had to be resolved, one way or another. Wiping her face, she grabbed her coat and scarf, and headed for the door. Allie had never been very brave, but now she had to know.

* * *

Louisa sat huddled in the red velvety armchair as Miss Craddock hurried into the library. She knew she should have insisted that the child go to bed. The girl now only looked more upset. Miss Craddock quickly picked up the shawl which Louisa had dropped.

'You mustn't sit here, you'll get a chill. Now come upstairs...'

Miss Craddock's gentle Scots burr was comfort itself, but Louisa resisted it and struggled up in her seat. She fixed her governess with her bright green eyes.

'Miss Craddock. Would you take me to London?'

Miss Craddock's kindly face registered surprise. She knew that would be impossible. She answered softly. 'Really Louisa, I don't think now is the time...'

But Louisa had already begun her attack, thinking quickly.

'I need some dresses. I've nothing fit to wear. And there are no decent dressmakers in the country! You've often said so yourself!'

Miss Craddock saw that the child was overwrought. She needed a good night's sleep, and perhaps a powder. There were some times a governess had to be firm.

'I'm sorry, Louisa. It's out of the question. No!'

Louisa looked at Miss Craddock, in despair.

The footman was filling the oil lamps in the hall, as Anthony raced straight down the stairs towards him, clutching a note. His manner was cool and brisk.

'Evans!' The tiny footman jumped. 'I shall want to send my baggage on ahead, to London. And see that this note is delivered to Miss Allegra Turner.'

And thrusting the note into the servant's hand, Anthony turned and hurried back up the stairs.

* * *

Roger, with the help of Fran, was up to his elbows in files, papers and documents. She turned to him with a plea. 'What is it we're looking for?'

Roger only knew one answer. 'Keep digging!'

Fran sighed, and she knew they'd be there till Doomsday if necessary. If only Roger had been a bee-keeper! But she persisted.

'What connection could these Hallams possibly have had with a *Prince of Wales*?'

Roger looked at his wife through raised eyebrows, noting her ignorance. '*The* Prince of Wales, Fran. *Bertie*. Edward VII! Any political or social link could be important. The Hallams were one of Rutland's most important families you know!'

While Roger was rabbiting on, Fran had found the sought-after file. She had opened it and started reading before Roger had taken notice.

'New readers begin here . . .'

Roger snatched the file from Fran, and began to read it out loud himself. After all, *he* was the historian.

'Captain Hallam's *resignation* from the army . . .?' Roger looked surprised. Very few army officers resigned after ten years' service. He went on. '. . . coincided with His Royal Highness' Edward, Prince of Wales' inspection of the regiment in Delhi on January 12, 1876 . . .'

Fran leaned back, thoughtfully. 'I wonder what *we* were doing then?'

Roger turned on Fran like a dog being stopped from enjoying his bone. He was not amused, but continued, 'On January 20, the regiment was posted to Lucknow, but *without* Captain Hallam, who returned to England at once . . .'

Roger's voice dropped to a mutter, as intrigued, he started reading the file to himself. Fran impatiently skimmed over his shoulder.

'A member of His Highness' entourage, one of his ladies in attendance, left the tour shortly afterwards . . .' Fran started to laugh, for the first time since they'd entered the newspaper office. She seemed delighted.

'Well, well, well! It would appear that Captain Hallam was indiscreet! With one of the Prince's girlfriends!'

Roger studied the file carefully. No wonder the records had been so difficult to find. Fran prodded Roger to read on.

'And it seems that Captain Hallam was forced to resign his Army Commission, after ten years of active service . . .'

'*Very* active!' Interrupted Fran.

'And the *whole* Hallam family were ostracised from *London* and its society . . .' Roger stopped reading. '*London*?'

Fran finished the sentence for him. 'And moved to Thornaby Hall, Rutland!'

She put down the file, and noticed that Roger was upset. She wondered what was the matter now. Roger exploded mildly.

'So they weren't even Rutlanders!'

Fran couldn't see where that made a difference. Roger could.

'None of this is any good for my research at all! What a waste!'

Fran was about to reply in annoyance when suddenly they heard someone calling from outside the room.

'Mum! Dad!'

Fran started to run to the door. That was Shaun. He burst into the room, out of breath and upset.

'Oh please help!'

Fran's face went white. She had never seen him so upset. 'Shaun, what is it?'

Shaun took a deep breath. 'It's Allie. I think she's been seeing a *ghost*!'

Roger looked as though he'd been slapped. 'That's impossible!'

But Shaun wasn't there for debates. Allie was panic-striken. And frightened. And he didn't know what to do . . .

Fran put an arm reassuringly round her son. 'Where is she, darling?'

'At the cottage. Do you think she'll be all right?'

Fran exchanged a look with Roger. They couldn't be sure, but they certainly weren't taking any chances. Roger pulled out his keys.

'Everybody into the car!'

Roger and Fran and Shaun raced out, Roger still holding the Hallam file.

When they arrived back at the cottage, the Burrs found it dark and deserted, Allie's bed a mess as she had left it. Roger dropped the files on the table as they looked round.

'She's gone!'

Fran didn't need a Professor of History to tell her that. She had more pressing worries.

'It's getting dark! Where could she be?'

They looked at each other, trying to think.

Allie crouched by some bushes, watching Thornaby Hall. She had arrived outside just in time to see the Water Board workers going home for the day. The last light had been switched off, and the workers had cycled and motored away just as the winter's early darkness was setting in.

Allie watched from her hiding place, cold and stiff, not sure what she was looking for. But then, as she stretched painfully, she saw a dim and flickering light go on in the front hall of Thornaby Hall.

* * *

Louisa carried the flickering lantern down the stairs and into the front hall. She moved silently, taking care not to trip over her long flowing nightdress, as the rest of the household slept. She reached the front door, then stopped and listened, and satisfied, opened the door, her hand quivering.

* * *

Allie watched the front door of Thornaby Hall open, but she could see nobody coming out. She waited for a moment, and thought she saw a light flickering, but she couldn't be sure. But Allie was sure as she saw the large oak door close once more, and the light, that thin wisp of light, seemed to appear again, and travel in the direction of the disused stables. She scrambled to her feet, and followed the elusive light to the old stables.

* * *

Louisa stood in her draughty nightdress in the stables, looking about fitfully. She put her glowing lantern down on a bench, and then slowly and painfully made her way over to the stall where Turk had been kept. She saw the pony's bridle, and picking it up gently, she pressed it to her cheek where it mingled with her tears and her long dark hair. She spoke gently, almost in a whisper, 'Oh Turk, what did they do to you?'

Suddenly she heard a sound come from outside.

Frightened, Louisa threw the bridle down. She ran silently in her bare feet to the lantern, and blew her light out.

* * *

The light in the disused stable went out as Allie approached, but she was near enough to find the stable door. Not seeing a soul, Allie carefully opened the stable door, its rusty hinges creaking in the still night. She shivered, and then taking her courage in both hands, slowly proceeded into the stables. As her eyes adjusted to the gloom, she inched forward only to find her way being suddenly and definitely blocked. Allie threw out her hands in horror, and felt the dozens of boxes and crates, put there by the Water Board who now used the stables as a storage house. Relieved, Allie started to look around when a light came on behind her, and she spun around, heart in her mouth. Roger was standing in the doorway, glaring. He shone his torch around the empty stables.

Back at the cottage Roger, Fran and Shaun gathered round Allie. She was desperately trying to get warm, which wasn't easy in the freezing cottage and with her father's cool reception.

'But what do you think you were doing?'

'Roger, please! Let her be!'

Fran handed Allie a steaming mug of cocoa which Allie took gratefully. She felt everyone's eyes on her as she sipped her drink.

'But she's been ghost-hunting!'

Fran sprang to Allie's defence. 'She hasn't—'

Allie for once contradicted her mother. She answered determinedly, 'I have!'

The Burrs looked at Allie with surprise, Shaun with admiration. 'Did you see anything?'

Allie nodded as Shaun waited eagerly. But Roger

couldn't hold himself back. He exploded, 'Alison, you know there are no such things as ghosts! Don't you?'

He looked at his daughter pleadingly. Fran broke in.

'Tell us what you saw.'

Allie put her mug onto the table, and tried to collect her facts as her father had always taught her. She began slowly. 'Well I've heard the name – *Louisa*.'

Shaun interrupted her, baffled. '*Louisa*?'

She took a deep breath and went on. 'And I've heard laughter and noises and gunshots and all sorts of things about the Hall and grounds!'

She looked at her father who seemed stunned, then annoyed. He dismissed it all.

'It must have been some of the Water Board people.'

Allie was emphatic. 'There was no one from the Water Board about!'

'Then you must have been imagining it.'

Fran immediately defended her daughter. 'Roger, Allie isn't given to fantasising!'

Roger looked at his family, incredulously.

'She's only heard some simple noises!' He finally said.

'And *seen* things!'

'And felt them!'

'And sensed them!' Allie now spoke up for herself. 'These incidents keep happening and I don't know *why*!'

Roger looked at Allie. She was so intense, so sure. He didn't understand her a bit. He wanted reasons; he wanted facts.

Now it was Fran's turn to explode. 'Reason be hanged! Allie is being terrified. Isn't that enough?'

Fran looked at her daughter and worried. Allie had become so thin, so pale. That was proof for her. 'There must be some facts somewhere! There must be a reason for all this!'

Roger nodded his head in approval. At last they were getting somewhere. Or so he thought until Fran continued.

'And if not in the present, then perhaps in the past!'

His face began to turn red, and Fran fancied she could see the smoke coming out of his ears. But she was going to have her say.

'Roger, it's not impossible! Just because you don't choose to acknowledge something doesn't mean it isn't so!'

Roger almost laughed at Fran. 'And you think your children know better?'

Fran answered resolutely. 'It wouldn't be the first time!'

Roger couldn't believe his ears. He had begun to wish he'd never got his research grant; he was beginning to wish he didn't have a family. He faced his wife.

'Fran! This whole business is getting crazy! If you're all going to carry on like this, I think we'd better head for home!'

Fran remembered that he had been disappointed with his research. 'Oh, tired of our little project, are we?'

They glared at each other. Allie couldn't bear to see her parents angry, especially if she were the cause. She tried one last desperate appeal. 'But if we go home now, then I'll never know!'

Roger turned to his daughter, and felt himself softening at her big blue eyes. He had to respect her sincerity though he despaired at her lack of reasoning. When he spoke, he tried to sound milder.

'Allie, there is nothing to know! Except that an active imagination in new surroundings sometimes plays funny tricks. Now, I think you've had upsets enough, and there's no point in our staying here any longer. So we're going home.'

Allie looked at him pleadingly, and even Fran looked disappointed. But Roger had the final say.

'We're going first thing in the morning!'

And Allie felt lost.

The next morning, Allie was up and dressed very early. She

was quietly packing some of her jeans and jumpers into a bag, when Roger came up noiselessly behind her. He was still in his pyjamas and dressing-gown, and spoke softly, as the rest of the family slept.

'Allie. I just wanted to say—'

Allie cut him short quietly, nodding towards Fran and Shaun. 'Sh! We'd best let the others sleep . . .'

Roger nodded, and then looked at his daughter for a moment, sadly. There was so much he wanted to say but couldn't. She had been his very own special little girl since she was a baby. He put out his hand, and uncharacteristically, stroked her hair. She looked up, and Roger withdrew his hand. He watched as Allie closed her small suitcase, lifted it off the table, and got ready to carry it out to the car. Roger sighed as Allie went outside, and then sat down and absently began to thumb through the Hallam files which were still on the table.

* * *

Anthony came down the stairs, very early in the morning, and accosted Evans the footman as he was carrying buckets of coal into the reception rooms. He was fastening his uniform jacket as he asked, 'Have there been any messages for me?'

Evans shook his head feeling more and more weighed down by the heavy buckets. But Anthony didn't detain him long. He headed towards the front door.

'Let me know if any arrive!'

And he strode out.

Louisa woke up with a start, and realised it was morning. As she threw back her covers, she saw her dirty bare feet and remembered her night trip to the stables. She also remembered that Anthony was leaving. Not bothering to find her wrap, Louisa flew to the bedroom door only to be met by Miss Craddock, who was coming for her. Miss Craddock was surprised by her appearance.

'And where do you think you're going?'

Louisa pushed her matted hair out of her eyes, and shivered in her flimsy nightdress. 'Has Anthony left yet?'

Miss Craddock spoke patiently as she herded Louisa back into the room. 'No, not yet! We've plenty of time. Let's come back in and dress.'

But Louisa had Anthony on her mind. 'I must speak to him!'

And Miss Craddock promised that she could. *After* she had dressed . . .

* * *

Roger sat at the shaky cottage table, listening to Fran and Shaun's quiet snores, as he leafed absently through the Hallams' files. He was waiting for Allie to come back in when suddenly a name caught his eye.

'*Louisa*? Louisa *Hallam*?'

Roger grabbed the file, and quickly read what he had found. Then he jumped up, and rushed over to his sleeping wife.

* * *

Allegra waited in the conservatory, alone and hesitant. Though it was fairly warm indoors, she did not remove her long brown overcoat, nor her straw boater. She started as the door to the garden flew open, and Anthony hurried inside to her. He was bright with the cold, but happy to see her.

'You received my note! I heard you were going to London. Have a seat.'

He motioned her to a chair, and went to take her wrap. But Allegra kept her coat.

'My Fraulein's still packing. I mustn't be long.'

'I know. But you couldn't disappear without us speaking again. And I wasn't sure when you were going.' Anthony smiled at Allegra. The girl returned his smile.

'Things have been rather difficult for me lately. But our meetings have meant a lot. I'll miss them.'

Allegra bowed her head, and said she was sorry they had to end. Anthony finally caught her eye, and asked, 'Do they?'

Allegra looked up at him, puzzled. She was going to London that day.

'But so am I.' Anthony explained. 'But it might be difficult to meet there at first.'

Allegra kept looking at Anthony, still puzzled, but now waiting. He didn't keep her in suspense for long.

'I think I have an idea.'

And Anthony smiled at Allegra.

Louisa hurried down the stairs, dressed now, but none too carefully. She was still trying to tie her hair ribbon as she looked around.

'Where's Anthony?'

Miss Craddock caught up with her, and hastily tied Louisa's hair ribbon. She answered the straining Louisa patiently.

'I think he was walking outside . . .'

And Louisa was out the door before Miss Craddock could check her shoebuttons.

* * *

Allie was outside, arranging her bags in the car when suddenly she heard, as if in the wind, '*Anthony*—'

She spun around, and then threw her hands over her ears. But it was no use. She heard faintly, once again, '*Anthony*!'

Allie lowered her hands, and looked round. She saw no one.

'Who is it?' She called softly, unsure. She chanced a question, '*Louisa*? Louisa is that *you*?'

Allie received no reply, but again sensed something, stronger than ever. She looked off towards the Hall and its grounds, but then turned back to the cottage again, torn. She knew she had to make up her own mind.

Allie pushed her suitcase into the car, then set out towards the Hall, drawn to the sound of Louisa's voice.

* * *

Anthony and Allegra sat on the conservatory bench, as Anthony spoke with conviction. 'So you see, there's still plenty of time! We could meet before we leave, without any trouble to anyone at all. What do you say?' He looked at Allegra, all charming and dashing in his uniform. Allegra thought for a moment, then shyly nodded her head. Anthony seized the reply.

'But where?'

Allegra thought for another moment. 'Our house?' she asked weakly.

'No.' Anthony was positive about that. He remembered, 'There's a small clearing by the quarry not far from where your parents live. Get your governess to tell you where it is.' Anthony waited for Allegra's nod, which came. 'We can meet there in an hour. You can't miss it. And if we've time, I might even be able to take you for a walk—'

'Oh how lovely!'

But Anthony was suddenly distracted by his father, who had just entered the conservatory through the library. Sir Reginald looked furious.

Anthony sprang to his feet, and prepared to face his father.

Louisa ran through the grounds of Thornaby Hall, looking for Anthony, shivering. She wished she'd brought her shawl, but finding Anthony was more important. Disappointed and miserable because she couldn't spot him anywhere, Louisa called Anthony's name one last time, and then headed through the garden towards the conservatory door.

Sir Reginald and Anthony faced each other in the conservatory; each tense, neither knowing what to say. Trying to maintain some semblance of dignity, Sir Reginald spoke first.

'I should have thought to have found my daughter in here. I heard a young girl's voice!'

He turned and stonily faced Allegra. Anthony immediately stepped forward to introduce them. Sir Reginald nodded formally, and then continued, 'If you are looking for my daughter, Miss Turner, I believe she's still in her room.' Sir Reginald returned his gaze to his son. 'I should like to have a word with you, please.'

Anthony, tight-lipped, told him that he had nothing really to say. Sir Reginald exploded like a rocket.

'Let me be the judge of that! I understand you're leaving! If you'd be so kind as to give me a few words!'

Anthony realised he had pushed his father too far. He nodded, and agreed to follow his father. But first, he turned back to Allegra, who was watching, her cheeks blushing.

'Would you like me to take you home?'

Allegra hastily shook her head as she drew her coat about her, and headed for the garden door. Sir Reginald watched, gritting his teeth.

Anthony held open the door for Allegra. As she passed, he whispered, 'I'll see you in an hour. At the quarry . . .'

Allegra hurried swiftly out of the room, her head down, her cheeks burning, without making a sign. Anthony watched her go. Sir Reginald looked at his son, and could restrain himself no longer. He opened the door leading into the library and barked, 'Would you kindly step in here, sir!'

Anthony saw the familiar fury on his father's face.

Allegra hurried out of Thornaby Hall, and out through the garden where Louisa lay in wait.

Louisa had been outside the conservatory door and heard every word that Anthony had said. She was determined to confront Allegra. She waited until Allegra had scurried away from the house, and then set off down the path after her.

* * *

Back at the cottage, Fran and Shaun, still in their pyjamas, huddled round Roger as he displayed the open file.

'Look at this,' he exclaimed. 'There *was* a Louisa! A Louisa Hallam! And she was Captain Anthony Hallam's youngest sister! She used to live at Thornaby Hall!' Roger turned to the now wide-awake Shaun. 'Call Allie!'

Shaun looked about dumbly. 'Where is she?'

'By the car, outside!'

And Shaun sped off to tell his sister the news.

Allie hurried down the country path, hearing nothing, seeing no one, and wondering if she'd done the right thing. The family might begin to miss her soon. She stopped by a clump of apple trees, which were just beginning to get their leaves, and checked the time. The family would still be sleeping. She had time. Allie continued down the country lane.

* * *

Allegra was walking very quickly down the country path leading towards her home. She was wondering how she would be able to slip away from her governess when she became aware of footsteps behind her. She paused for a moment, and listened. But hearing nothing, she convinced herself that it was only her imagination, though now she walked all the faster, towards a fork in the road.

Louisa raced down the dusty path, cursing the headstart she had given Allegra. She looked round, and noticed a shortcut which would bring her past the fork in the road before Allegra. Gathering her trailing skirts, Louisa headed off down the path, passing some budding saplings on the way. Her spirits surged as she drew nearer.

* * *

Allie came to the fork in the road and paused, wondering which way to go. Just as she'd decided on a path, she was stopped short as she heard a faint and dreamlike voice call, '*Allegra*!'

Allie looked desperately round, and tried to hurry towards the sound of the voice. It seemed to come from the bushes, then the trees. She raced down the path, and rounded a bend and suddenly she saw a girl, in a long brown overcoat with a straw boater, looking hesitantly around her, as if called. Allie stopped in amazement. The girl was an exact double of *her*. Allie watched horrified as the girl's large blue eyes, piercing and so like her own, scanned the area, looking, and yet not seeing her. Then the nervous figure gathered up her skirts, and raced as quickly as she could down the path. It was like watching an echo, a dream. It was a crazy reflection. Allie at last cried out, 'Oh! Who are you?'

But the figure was swiftly disappearing. Allie pulled herself together, and followed quickly in her double's wake.

'Let me speak to you! Wait!'

But the elusive young lady rounded a bend, which Allie recognised led to the church. As soon as the figure disappeared round it, Allie followed; but round the turning,

Allie saw no double or figure; just an empty, open graveyard which sheltered at the foot of the church. She raced in and searched, but could find nothing save a cluster of old and neglected gravestones. As she looked about in despair, she became aware of car and traffic noises coming from somewhere in the distance. Her eye fell on one of the gravestones; one of the oldest and most neglected of the lot. She drew closer, and read the inscription, and then cried out in horror, 'Oh no! You mustn't go!'

Allie spun away from the gravestone, crying.

Fran and Roger were still in their dressing-gowns, poring over the Hallam files, when Shaun ran back into the cottage, breathless.

'Allie's not anywhere about!'

Fran and Roger faced their son, surprised.

'Are you *sure*?'

Shaun nodded his head. Fran turned to Roger, concerned. 'Now where could she possibly be?'

Roger was transfixed by a page he was reading. His answer was short. 'Thornaby Hall.'

Fran looked at her husband, puzzled. Roger thrust the paper he was reading in front of his wife.

'Have a look at that!'

Fran's face was clouded, then worried, as she studied the file. Shaun tried to see what it said. Roger shot up, hastily.

'Come on everybody. Get dressed!'

Shaun watched in amazement as his parents started pulling on whatever clothes were close to hand. He was still bewilderingly in the dark. 'But why?'

Roger's voice was terse as he pulled the jumper over his head.

'We've got to find Allie!'

Shaun moved as quickly as he could.

6
The Quarry

Shaun tried to find out what was happening as he and Fran and Roger struggled into their last pieces of clothing, but his parents proved no help.

'It might be absolutely nothing at all,' reassured Fran. 'Just a storm in a tea-cup.'

'Or it might not be?'

Fran and Roger stopped dressing for a moment, and stared at their son. They then went back to their boots and their jackets. But Shaun had finished dressing, and persisted.

'But what does all this have to do with *Allie*? And the alleged Louisa?'

Fran tried to remain calm. 'We're not certain. But we're going to find out!'

Shaun was more baffled than ever. 'But that Louisa lived a hundred years ago!' Shaun turned to his father. 'And I thought you didn't believe in that sort of thing!'

Roger's mouth set in a firm line.

'Call it caution if you like,' he said, looking for the car keys.

'You mean it's better safe than sorry?'

Roger had heard enough. For the first time, he realised he was rather tense and nervous. He flung open the cottage door.

'Come on everybody! To the Hall. Let's find Allie!'

They all rushed out, but not nearly fast enough for Roger.

* * *

Anthony stormed out of the library, his interview with his

father over. He was furious, unused to being spoken to by anyone so harshly, and he was determined not to repeat the experience. He would be very glad to leave his father's house, and he wished he'd gone straight to London in the first place. He was so tense and preoccupied that he did not at first notice Miss Craddock, who was waiting worriedly in the hallway.

'Captain Anthony, have you seen Louisa?'

Anthony looked through her as if she wasn't there. Why did everyone seem to think he was a wet-nurse and a nanny? Miss Craddock went on, anxiously.

'Louisa went out before. Looking for you. Didn't you see her?'

Anthony shook his head, short and bad-tempered. 'I was with my father! Evidently not.'

Miss Craddock looked as if she'd been wounded. Anthony felt immediately ashamed. Craddie had never been anything less than good and kind to him.

'Oh, I'm sorry, Miss Craddock. But I'm sure she'll be around here somewhere.' He smiled weakly. 'Hiding from her lessons.'

Miss Craddock nodded and prepared to go. But before she did, she had to ask Anthony one last thing.

'Captain Anthony. Is it true you're going to be leaving us again?'

Miss Craddock's warm brown eyes stared up at him, and Anthony felt surprised that the news had got out so quickly. He answered honestly.

'Yes, soon. Very soon.'

Miss Craddock nodded understandingly. 'Are you going back to your regiment?'

Anthony tried not to smile, and looked at his old nanny fondly. 'Hardly, Craddie. No. And I'm not sure when I'll be back.' Anthony's mind flew to another thought. 'But you'll look after Louisa for me, won't you?'

Miss Craddock nodded her head very firmly.

Louisa ran along the path, a little way from the church, tired and distraught. She had not caught up with Allegra, she hadn't even caught a glimpse of her. She felt hot, and her hair was straggly, and her ribbons were once again undone. She stumbled and began to cry as she grew tired.

'Oh Anthony! Why did you choose *Allegra*?'

There was only one thing to be done. She had to stop Anthony and Allegra. She headed towards the quarry.

Anthony and Miss Craddock moved to another corner in the hallway as Mary, the tweeny, passed carrying fresh linen. They waited till she'd gone up the stairs.

'Oh, Captain Anthony,' Miss Craddock started again. 'Must you go? Your family will be so disappointed!'

Anthony looked warmly at Miss Craddock. She was the only one who felt that way. It was best that he should leave.

But his old governess persisted. 'Where will you go?'

'London. My club. You needn't worry about me, Craddie.' Anthony gently mimicked her warm Scots accent. 'I'm no longer your wee charge!'

Miss Craddock smiled, and Anthony thought how sorry he'd be to say goodbye to his old nanny again, and Louisa.

'I'd like to be able to see Louisa sometime, if you come up to London.'

Miss Craddock sensed that if she did that, it would be without their parents' permission. She nodded her head slowly. Anthony was grateful.

'And it'll be good to see you too.' Anthony gave her one last smile. 'But I suppose you'll have to *find* Louisa first!'

Miss Craddock remembered her mission, and started to bustle away. 'Yes. You'll be wanting to say goodbye!'

Anthony stood in the hall, deep in thought as he remembered his plans.

'There's no rush. There's something I must do first. I shan't be leaving till later. I can say goodbye to her then!'

He turned and hurried up the stairs.

Allegra hastened along the dusty lane, then feeling tired, stopped, and looked at her watch. The walk between the two houses was taking her longer than she had thought. She decided not to go straight back to her house, and possibly her Fraulein's awkward questions, but headed straight towards the clearing near the quarry instead.

* * *

Roger, Fran and Shaun raced back to the dilapidated old cottage almost as quickly as they had left it. Fran sped past the other two, and grabbed a notebook and a pencil which lay scattered on the table. She set to writing furiously. Shaun came to peer over her shoulder.

'Can't you write any faster?'

Roger quickly came to Fran's rescue. 'Leave your Mother be, Shaun! She's right! It's a good idea to leave a note in case Allie comes back first!'

Fran finished her note, and ripped it from the book. She held it up, and looked around.

'Now to leave it somewhere Allie can find it!'

Shaun grabbed the note and propped it in front of their beloved portable telly. Roger motioned impatiently, and the three Burrs raced back out of the cottage.

* * *

Allie had never felt so lost in her life. She stared round the graveyard, distraught; not really certain who or what she wanted to see. She felt confused, and torn. She felt as if she had found an answer, but was still looking for the question. She felt she *had* to find Louisa. She called out.

'Louisa! Louisa, answer me! I'm trying to help!'

But it was to no avail. All Allie heard was the sound of her own voice.

Shaun, closely followed by his parents, hurried into Thornaby Hall's front hall and looked around.

'Hello! Is anybody home?'

The three Burrs explored the front hall, but saw nothing save the Water Board's usual glaring lighting, posters, and odd table and chair. None of the Water Board workers' hats or coats were about. Roger spoke frustratedly. 'Isn't this typical? Don't tell me nobody's here!'

The ginger-haired caretaker, broom half-heartedly in hand, entered right behind the Burrs. He sighed. He'd hoped that this was going to be a quiet day. He addressed them indifferently.

'Can I help you?'

Fran turned to him gratefully. Her words came out in a rush. 'We're looking for our daughter, Allie. We're the family that's staying at the cottage.'

Some of Fran's words penetrated the caretaker's mind. Allie? That would be that polite young girl, the one with the big blue eyes, who helped him collect the litter when he was sweeping the grounds. You didn't meet many polite young people like that nowadays. The caretaker was pleasantly lost in his thoughts. Roger quickly interrupted him.

'Have you seen her?'

The caretaker shook his ginger head. Roger continued impatiently.

'But she's missing. Do you mind if we have a look around?'

The caretaker was startled out of his reverie.

'*Missing*, did you say?'

The caretaker felt genuinely sorry. He had liked the girl. Roger sprang into action.

'I think we should split up. I'll take upstairs; Fran you take downstairs and Shaun, you look outside!'

Each Burr immediately followed their command. Roger dashed up the stairs, Fran hurried to the library, and Shaun flew to the side exit. The caretaker was left on his own, but it took a minute until he noticed. He panicked, and ran after Roger.

'Wait! I'll give you a hand!'

And the caretaker disappeared up the mahogany staircase.

Fran looked around what was once the library frantically. Originally the heart of Thornaby Hall, it had now been converted into yet more offices for the Water Board workers. The room had been partitioned off into various cubicles, with a Water Board desk in each one, and she searched each cubicle carefully. As she moved her voice echoed in the carpetless room.

'Allie? *Allie*?'

But Allie was nowhere to be seen.

Allie stood outside the quiet church, not knowing what to do. Her family would be up soon, and she should be turning back. She had very little to go on, but still felt she couldn't give up. Suddenly she spotted a light going on in the church itself. Feeling strengthened by the light, Allie turned and hurried into the church.

She rushed into the church just as the vicar was surveying the plasterers' work of the day before. He wondered if the Sistine Chapel had taken this long. As he pushed his glasses back up the bridge of his nose, he seemed surprised to see young Allie standing there, pale and breathless. He smiled at her.

'Oh hello! You're one of the Burr flock, aren't you?' Somehow he didn't expect to see them at any of his services. 'Now what can I do for you?'

Allie fixed him with her large blue eyes. 'Have you seen a *girl* about outside? Or anyone?'

The vicar thought for a moment, then positively shook his head. 'No, it's been as quiet as the proverbial graveyard. Whom are you looking for?'

He looked down at Allie kindly, and she tried to act nonchalant. 'Would you know anything about a Hallam, a Louisa Hallam?'

The name struck a familiar chord with the vicar. 'Ah, the Hallams?' Allie looked up hopefully. The vicar continued. 'Haven't your family traced them yet? I must say I admire your father's persistence! Rather like Daniel and his lions!'

The vicar stopped and considered that story for a minute. He needed a sermon for this Sunday. Allie persisted. 'But do you?'

The vicar turned back to the inquisitive girl. Questions must run in their family.

'No, I'm afraid not. I don't know any more than I've already told you.'

But Allie couldn't let it be. 'Then a *quarry*. Do you know where there's a quarry?'

The vicar brightened. There he could be of some help. He told Allie about a disused quarry, about a mile from his church. She started off immediately, and raced out his door.

'Thank you very much!'

The vicar was perplexed. Why ever did she want to go there? He called after her, but it was too late. Allie had already gone. He turned back to the plasterwork, shaking his head. 'Ah. Stony ground . . .'

The vicar cheered up again suddenly. 'Stony ground!'

At last he had the topic for this week's sermon.

Roger entered one of the Hall's upstairs rooms, pushing cobwebs out of his way as he went. He could see that this had once been a child's nursery, by its small brass bed and ancient rocking horse, which were now partially covered with dust cloths. Roger quickly scanned the room, but seeing no Allie was about to pull his head out again when suddenly his eye rested on something in the corner. Looking closer, Roger was immediately amazed, and upset. He called for Fran. The ginger-haired caretaker came ambling in instead.

'You won't find her in here,' he puffed. 'Not even *I* come in here . . .'

The caretaker stopped short as he saw what Roger was looking at. But before he could find his voice, Fran came rushing into the room.

'Is Allie here? Have you found her?'

But in less than a moment, Fran too was silent. Now they wanted to find Allie more than ever.

* * *

Louisa arrived at the clearing by the quarry, her long skirt now dusty and dirty; her hair awry. She brushed the matted hair out of her eyes as she looked around. But all she saw was the barren, flat land which led to the stony quarry. There was no sign of Anthony, or Allegra. At least not yet. Louisa decided to shelter behind a nearby, large, craggy rock, and wait for Allegra. For Louisa was sure that she was on her way.

* * *

Allie hurried along the uneven road in the countryside, following the directions that the vicar had given her. She was tired, and thirsty and her feet ached, but she felt she had to find the quarry. She hoped that it really *would* be disused when she got there. She hoped that she could then forget about all this, and return home, with her family. But above all, she hoped that that gravestone in the churchyard could be proved wrong.

Fran's hand reached out for Roger's as she tried to make sense out of what she was seeing in the nursery. For once, the vibrant Fran seemed pale, and unsteady.

'Oh Roger! You don't think Allie knows, do you?'

Roger wasn't sure what to reply, and he was spared the trouble as they heard Shaun's voice in the hall outside.

'We're in here, darling!'

Shaun heard his mother's voice, and gratefully bounded into the small, close nursery. His words came out in a tumble.

'Allie's been seen!'

'Where?'

Shaun collected his thoughts. 'At the church. Not long ago. She spoke to the vicar. Asking about some quarry—'

The caretaker cut him short, puzzled by the information. That quarry was all played out, and hadn't been used in years. Why would that nice young girl want to go there?

Roger was too impatient to guess. They would have to find that out when they got there. Right now, he only wanted to know one thing.

'Which way is the quarry?'

The three Burrs crowded around the Water Board map in Thornaby Hall's front hall, trying to trace the quarry. They were not helped by the concerned caretaker, who was now breathing over their shoulders. Fran felt almost desperate.

'What does a quarry *look* like?'

The caretaker's stubby finger landed straight on the map.

'That. It's by that clearing, about a couple of miles from here!'

Roger was running out of the door almost before the caretaker had finished his sentence.

'I'll get the car!'

Fran and Shaun turned back to the map, and waited.

* * *

Anthony had left Thornaby Hall, and was heading across the grounds on his way to the clearing. As he hurried through the gardens, and then passed the stables and paddock, he was rather inconvenienced by a parcel he was carrying. The package was large and flat, and about two feet square, and had been hastily wrapped with brown paper and string. He juggled the parcel once again, and was happy that, for once, no one had witnessed him leaving Thornaby Hall.

Allegra arrived at the clearing near the quarry, the one that Anthony had described to her. She glanced round, but all she saw was the flat, uninteresting land, accented by a few large rocks. She felt nervous, and even a bit annoyed that Anthony hadn't shown up yet, though she was undoubtedly early. Allegra looked at the watch which was pinned to her dress, and vowed only to wait a few minutes, or she would be bound to be missed. She made her way towards a large, craggy rock to sit and wait.

* * *

Allie reached the clearing near the quarry, and though she found nothing extraordinary or strange, it did nothing to quieten her nerves. Her eyes darted about, but all she saw were the normal signs of modern civilisation. Scattered round the disused quarry she saw rusty beer cans, the odd coke tin, and bits and pieces of paper and litter. Some vandals had scribbled graffiti on a large rock nearby. Some old cables and wires blew in the wind. She looked desperately about.

'*Louisa*! Are you here?'

But Allie could see or hear nothing.

* * *

Allegra grew uneasy as she approached the large rock. She wished she'd never agreed to meet with Anthony; she was old enough to know she shouldn't. Allegra's back stiffened as she decided to slip away. Anthony hadn't come yet, and no harm would be done. But before she went, she tried one last time, 'Anthony?'

Still no reply, but before Allegra could start on her way, Louisa stepped out from behind the rock, and smiled at Allegra.

* * *

Fran and Shaun waited impatiently in Thornaby Hall eager for Roger to come. The caretaker hovered over them annoyingly. Fran stared out of the front window.

'Oh where's Roger? What's taking him so long with the car?'

The caretaker, now pacing nervously, suddenly stopped in his tracks, his hand flying up to hit his forehead. He said frantically, 'I must have closed the car park!'

Fran looked at him as she had seldom looked at a fellow human being before, and then, without exchanging a word, they bolted for the car park.

* * *

Louisa faced Allegra calmly, smiling and friendly. Allegra was surprised and uneasy. She started a bit as Louisa stood before her.

'What are you doing here?'

Louisa smiled at her charmingly, as if they met there every day of their lives for tea. 'You seem surprised! Anthony's going to be late. He's asked me to meet you and tell you!'

Allegra still felt nervous, and decided to start away. She had had more than enough of the Hallams. Louisa wouldn't hear of her going.

'Nonsense! He won't be long! And he'd be ever so hurt if you didn't wait, wouldn't he?'

Louisa placed her hand on Allegra's arm as she felt her

backing away. Allegra tried to turn, but Louisa tightened her hold on her companion's arm. Allegra stumbled.

'Oh!'

Louisa hastened to help her up.

* * *

Allie, standing in the empty clearing, was by now completely disheartened. She kicked at an old coke tin, and was about to give up, when suddenly she heard, as if carried on the wind, '*Oh*!'

But all Allie heard now was the rattle of the old coke tin as she spun around.

* * *

Louisa helpfully steadied Allegra as the girl regained her balance. She let go of her arm as Allegra brushed off her skirt.

'I'm sorry. Let's do be careful!'

Allegra silently nodded her head, and refused any further assistance. Louisa went on chatting happily.

'You know, Anthony said he'd like to take us for a walk! He promised. And he said we were to meet him. Right by the old quarry.'

Allegra looked hesitant, but Louisa didn't give her much time to think. 'Oh don't be such an old rabbit! You've plenty of time! Besides, you'll be leaving soon . . .'

Louisa's thoughts were suddenly a thousand miles away. Yes, Allegra would be leaving soon. And so would Anthony. She turned back to Allegra, and gently took her arm, smiling.

'So do come along! There's a lovely view! And they say it's ever so much nicer by the quarry. Shall we?'

And Louisa, holding Allegra's arm, walked on in the

direction of the quarry. Their footsteps began to crunch more and more as they neared the quarry's gravelly surface. Allegra began to feel afraid.

* * *

Allie tried to trace the direction from which the voice came, but it was like trying to catch the wind. She stood still, and listened to her own sigh, when she suddenly heard a crunching sound, a faraway sound. It came from the direction of the quarry. She started towards the sound.

* * *

Allegra and Louisa had reached the actual site of the quarry. It was large, forbidding, and grey, with a sheer drop that made Allegra shiver. She carefully stopped well clear of the quarry and its jagged rocks. Louisa simply smiled at Allegra, and went to stand nearer the quarry's edge. There was something about its terrifying nature that appealed to her.

'Just look at those rocks!'

Louisa's eyes gleamed as she faced the irregular, jagged side of the quarry face. She picked up a stone, and tossed it over the side, and then watched it fall, delighted. She turned to the uneasy Allegra.

'Miss Craddock would say that was *gravity*, but I think it's just fate, don't you?'

Allegra didn't know how to answer Louisa. She thought she was mad. She wanted to get away.

Louisa turned and picked up another stone. With a slow smile, she threw it over the side of the quarry. Louisa laughed.

* * *

Allie was hurrying towards the quarry when she thought she heard something drop, not far away. It was like stones, or pebbles being thrown. She quickened her pace, and began to run towards the quarry. She ran so fast and was so involved, she didn't notice her parents' car driving up behind her towards the clearing.

* * *

Anthony raced to the clearing, trying not to be late. He knew that Allegra wouldn't wait, if she came at all. When he finally reached the clearing, he looked quickly around. He saw nothing but the occasional rock, and tree. He rested his package on the ground, prepared for a short wait, when suddenly he heard sounds coming from the direction of the quarry. Smiling, he picked up his hastily wrapped parcel, and started towards the quarry.

Louisa stood, gazing down into the quarry, her back still to Allegra. She couldn't see why Allegra wouldn't join her at the quarry's edge. It was so breathtaking and exciting. Finally she snapped.

'Don't be such a goose, Allegra! I said it was perfectly all right! Come on!'

That was the cue Allegra had been waiting for. She'd had enough.

'I think I'd better be going!'

She picked up her trailing skirts, and turned away when suddenly she saw Anthony emerging from the clearing, carrying a brown paper parcel. She stopped as he saw her and smiled.

'Allegra! I looked for you by the clearing! I'm sorry I'm late!'

Anthony was pleased and rather surprised that she had come at all. He started towards Allegra, and then saw

Louisa, by the quarry, for the first time. He seemed taken aback, but not unkindly so. He turned to his younger sister. 'Louisa. What are you doing here?'

Louisa looked at Anthony speechless. Then suddenly all the fear that Allegra had felt came to the fore, and she ran towards Anthony for safety, for help. She desperately wanted to be taken away.

'Anthony!'

Louisa saw Allegra run towards her brother, and all her hatred for the girl welled up inside her. Allegra was *not* going to go to her brother. She tried to stop her.

'Allegra, *no*!'

She reached out to grab Allegra, to stop her for once and for all from ruining her life. But as Louisa grabbed out, she suddenly lost her uneasy foothold. She stumbled by the side of the quarry. 'Oh help!'

Anthony dropped his parcel, and ran towards Louisa.

* * *

'Oh help!'

Allie heard the words as clearly as if she were standing there. She raced to the site of the quarry, and suddenly she *was* there; an onlooker. She watched with horror; terror quickly overtaking her, as a soldier in Victorian clothes ran towards a young girl who was falling.

* * *

Louisa began to topple over the quarry's edge.

'Oh Anthony! Help!'

Anthony, and then Allegra ran to the quarry's side. Louisa had thrust her hand out, beseechingly; Anthony tried with all his might to catch her, but he was too late. Louisa tumbled into the dark and forbidding pit. Anthony and Allegra watched in terror. Then Allegra began to scream.

Anthony tore away, and raced towards the bottom of the quarry, horror-struck. *Louisa. Louisa*! Allegra pulled herself together and quickly followed.

* * *

Allie watched this double of herself as the young Victorian girl painstakingly made her way down into the quarry with the soldier. She was terrified, and sick, and turned her head away as the soldier and the young girl came across the still figure.

* * *

Anthony and Allegra made their way to Louisa, who was lying there, still. Anthony bent down and held her tightly in his arms. She was silent and limp as Anthony tried to feel for a heartbeat, distraught. He could find nothing. He just cradled Louisa tightly and wept.

* * *

The tears poured down from Allie's face as she turned away from the quarry, sobbing. She felt herself screaming as she ran.

'No! I tried to stop her. *No*!'

She suddenly found herself engulfed in arms, warm and caring arms which wrapped around her as she struggled.

'I tried to save her!'

'My darling, it's all right . . .'

Allie looked up to see her mother, warm and wonderful Fran, staring down at her protectively. Roger and Shaun were also huddling close. Allie spoke again.

'I did try to save her!'

Fran tried to brush away her daughter's tears, but looked down at her, truly agonised. At last she found her voice.

'Allie. You *couldn't*. You couldn't have saved her.'

And they led the sobbing Allie back to the car.

Roger, Fran and Shaun led a shaken and upset Allie back into Thornaby Hall. Roger had never seen Allie like this before, and found it difficult to comfort her. Fran spoke up.

'Allie, love, you couldn't have done anything!'

Allie didn't want to believe it. She had been *there*; she had *seen*. Fran tried to explain.

'It all happened over a hundred years ago. It happened in the past. And you can't change the past.'

'Then why did I see it? And I did see it!'

Fran knew that her daughter had seen it, and she knew where the answer might lie.

'Perhaps someone was trying to tell you something. Do you think you could come upstairs?'

Allie looked confused, but she followed her mother, her brother and her father up the stairs.

As the family entered the dusty dim nursery, Allie was immediately struck by a portrait, an unfinished portrait, propped up in the corner. And when she ventured close enough she could see it was a painting of her Victorian double, which had never been finished. The large blue painted eyes stared out at them from the portrait.

'But who was she?'

This had been the girl Allie had seen in the gardens, and at the quarry. She was confused and upset. Shaun hesitated, and then spoke.

'Mum's family came from around here.'

Fran took over. 'You certainly seem to have developed some sort of sixth sense about her. And her life . . . It's as if you were drawn to her; sensed her danger. As if you *had* to see everything that happened at that quarry!'

Allie was as muddled as Roger was full of contempt. He dismissed the theory as quickly as Allie grabbed at it.

'But *why*? I still don't understand *why*!'

Fran couldn't be sure herself. She was floundering. But there might only be one possible explanation. 'To learn the truth?'

'About *Louisa*?'

'Louisa *Hallam*.' Fran tried to explain to her daughter. 'We discovered something when looking through the files. Look at the signature. The portrait's signature.'

Allie and Shaun huddled round the portrait, and read the old, scrawled signature with difficulty.

'Hallam. Anthony Hallam.'

Fran began to get excited as she talked. 'Captain Hallam was Louisa's eldest brother. But he had been meeting with this girl, Allegra. He had been painting her portrait – *this* portrait!'

Allie's mind raced ahead. 'But others may have thought differently. Including Louisa!' Fran continued.

'So perhaps that's why she went to the quarry. She was jealous! And Allegra felt she was the cause! So perhaps Allegra's been trying to make her peace, for the wrong she did to Louisa, for all these years! So the ghost could finally be laid! It all makes sense. Don't you see?'

Fran turned towards her family, excited. Roger was slowly getting crosser. He had never heard such utter rubbish in his whole life.

'That's absolute rubbish! We found that information in an old newspaper. Allie could have done the same!'

Fran was immediately defensive.

'But she wasn't with us!'

Roger shook his head impatiently. He was desperately trying to apply logic to the whole situation. He wished Fran would try to do the same.

'All right, she wasn't! But if not *now*, then perhaps at some other time. After all, we've certainly got more than our share of history bumph at home!'

Roger tried to collect his thoughts as he fumbled for an explanation. 'Allie could have come across the information whilst flipping through some old papers, or in an old book! Or in one of her own history projects!' His daughter had a fertile imagination, who could say?

Allie tried to speak up. 'But I saw it all!'

'You *think* you did!'

'I *know* I did!' Allie was adamant now. She knew what she had seen and she'd never forget that sight. Fran agreed with Allie.

'Roger, there are certain things on heaven and earth that just can't be explained!'

Roger looked at his family, disturbed and uncomfortable. He loved them all so much. Yet how could he be asked to accept something he couldn't believe in? Allie's big blue eyes turned to him beseechingly, yet full of faith. He wanted to answer, but the ginger-haired caretaker made his way into the nursery.

'Have you seen enough now? I think we should close up. You've found the little lady. That's the important thing.'

Roger looked at his daughter, and realised he was right. Allie *was* the important thing. Roger held out his hand.

'Would you like to go home now?'

Allie nodded her head vigorously. She couldn't think of anywhere she would rather be.

Roger put his arm around her, and then spoke to his family. 'Come. We have a long drive.'

The caretaker was putting a dustcover over the portrait as the Burrs started out. Shaun turned back. He was struck by a sudden thought.

'*I* wonder if *I* have a double?'

Roger, Fran and Allie reacted as if all were struck by a single thought.

'*Urgh*!'

'What a gruesome thought!' Roger smiled. 'Horrifying!'

And the Burrs walked out of the nursery, Shaun highly offended. The caretaker hurried to join them, closing the door behind them.

The portrait was left alone in the empty room. The dustcover, not having been properly secured, began to slip down away from the painting. Once again, the portrait's eyes, so startling, so blue, could be seen, piercing through the room. Only this time, the portrait's eyes seemed to be at rest.

We hope you have enjoyed this Beaver Book. Here are some of the other titles:

Maggie Four lively books about Maggie McKinley, the irrepressible Glasgow teenager who determines to live her own life despite problems with her family and her over-enthusiastic boyfriend, James. The books are called *The Clearance*, *The Resettling*, *The Pilgrimage* and *The Reunion*; written by Joan Lingard, they were the basis for the TV series *Maggie*, and will be thoroughly enjoyed by all older readers

The Young Rider A must for all readers who love horses and ponies, this book explains all the basic principles of horsemastership – from choosing and buying a pony to caring for it and riding it. Written by Robert Owen and John Bullock, *The Young Rider* is illustrated throughout with line drawings

You may also enjoy some of the titles on our adult list such as:

Girl! Frank, lively and fun to read, this is an essential guide to teenage survival in the 1980s, with sensible, up-to-date advice on how to cope with parents, boyfriends, parties, sex, exams, jobs – and all the other things that can make life so complicated and confusing. Written by Barbara Brandenburger and Jennifer Curry, and illustrated with line drawings

These and many other Beavers are available from your local bookshop or newsagent, or can be ordered direct from: Hamlyn Paperback Cash Sales, PO Box 11, Falmouth, Cornwall TR10 9EN. Send a cheque or postal order, made payable to the Hamlyn Publishing Group, for the price of the book plus postage at the following rates:
UK: 40p for the first book, 18p for the second book, and 13p for each additional book ordered to a maximum charge of £1.49;
BFPO and Eire: 40p for the first book, 18p for the second book, plus 13p per copy for the next 7 books and thereafter 7p per book;
OVERSEAS: 60p for the first book and 18p for each extra book.

New Beavers are published every month and if you would like the *Beaver Bulletin*, a newsletter which tells you about new books and gives a complete list of titles and prices, send a large stamped addressed envelope to:

Beaver Bulletin
Hamlyn Paperbacks
Banda House
Cambridge Grove
London W6 0LE

204332